SHETLAND SHEEPDOGS TODAY

MAURICE BAKER

RINGPRESS

Acknowledgements

The author wishes to acknowledge the help and support of

Dr Karin Riemann (Germany)

Ingrid Myklebostad (Norway)

Ralph Martin

Bob Richman

Sheila Ann Baker — No 1 supporter and critic

An imprint of Ringpress Ltd.,
Spirella House, Letchworth, Hertfordshire SG6 4ET

First published 1988

ISBN No 0 948955 40 6

Production consultants: Landmark Ltd.
Typeset by Area News Ltd., Letchworth, Herts
Printed and bound in Great Britain by The Bath Press

Contents

Foreword

It is with pleasure that I pen the foreword for this the latest book on the shetland sheepdog. Like Jim Saunders before him Maurice Baker was a shipbuilder for most of his working days, he studied naval architecture and until recently was a chief draughtsman and senior manager with British Shipbuilders. He acquired his first sheltie, a Helensdale in 1955 and it was through our mutual friendship with Jim (Helensdale) Saunders that Maurice and I first met and perhaps because of our interest in the Helensdales we seemed to see shelties through similar eyes and still do.

Doshell Naiad, Challenge Certificate winner a great favourite owned by Margaret Dobson.

Maurice and Sheila's Ellendale/Shemaur kennel is well known both in the UK and overseas. The inmates are renowned for quality, their show presentation is perfection, and they have been exported to nine different countries.

Maurice's profession and judging ability have brought the opportunity to travel to many countries. I have judged with him abroad and he is a great amabassador for the breed. He has worked and judged throughout Scandinavia, Norway in particular, where he has studied the language and has almost been adopted as a native. This has given him quite an insight into the type and quality of the Scandinavian shelties which comes out clearly in the book.

During the past thirty years his dedication to the shetland sheepdog cannot be denied. He was a founder member and past chairman of the Northern Counties Shetland Sheepdog Club, and a founder member and past president of the Yorkshire Shetland Sheepdog Club and his experience makes this book commendable to anyone interested in shetland sheepdogs. It covers most aspects to assist the pet owner, new breeders and novice exhibitors as well as stirring the memory of the seasoned breeders. The best dogs section is an innovation which will bring to life for the newcomers some of the famous dogs who were perhaps just names on a pedigree.

Margaret Dobson (Doshell)

Introduction

THE shetland sheepdog or sheltie is surely one of the breeds which has adapted most successfully to the modern way of life. If you live in a suburban semi, a cottage or a country mansion, it will fit in without difficulty. It is small but not a toy, it is intelligent and lively, yet does not need miles of exercise, and despite its long coat simple brushing, combing and the occasional bath will suffice. It is all in all, an ideal companion and house dog.

The evolution and development of the shetland sheepdog from its early days as a crofters dog on the Shetland Isles, is like an ancient folk story. The islands stretch out northwards towards the polar circle and the land of the midnight sun, and were first inhabited almost 5,000 years ago. They are scattered with the remains of neolithic settlements and over the years people of many divergent cultures have settled there, not least of which were the Vikings. In fact, many of the old Norse customs and words are still in use on the islands today. Back in those far off days the little nondescript shetland sheepdog would guard his master's croft and herd the hardy sheep which grazed the rocky terrain of the windswept islands. In the course of the herding they kept the sheep away from the towns and it was this work which earned the sheltie the name of 'toonie' dog, and is probably the reason they can give tongue so easily even today.

A number of breeds of dogs visited the islands and were crossed with the sheltie and appear to have had some effect on the breed, many of their respective characteristics still cropping up today. So much so, that shelties have been called highly bred mongrels. We can trace points of colour to the cavalier king charles spaniel and their toy size, small pricked ears, and high set tails can be partly laid at the door of the pomeranian. The yakki dogs carried on board the Icelandic fishing boats which frequently visited the islands were of the spitz type with pricked ears, smutty muzzles, tails set high and carried plume-like over the back. One of their ancestors was probably the Norwegian buhund, a general farm dog of creamy buff colour who could easily be responsible for the wheaten colour with its superb pigmentation which occasionally appears. This colour is not a fault and shetland sheepdog enthusiasts either love it or hate it. My first sheltie Edana of Ellendale was purchased for ten guineas in 1954 from the legendary Jim Saunders (Helensdale), who later became my mentor. She was a wheaten, though when in full coat she had the most delicate tinge of gold, so naturally I love the colour providing it is not too wishy washy.

The geographical position of the Shetland Isles, exposed to the Atlantic gales meant that the dogs had to be hardy, and active in order to do the job of guarding and herding. The islands' location also brings links with the myths and legends of Scandinavia and it is easy to imagine why the sheltie is often referred to as the peerie or fairy dog in its native home.

The cross with the rough collie was the first positive step in an attempt to establish type in the breed in the early days and it is the keystone to the sheltie as we know it today.

I had dabbled in a few breeds prior to owning a sheltie, Scottish terriers, wire fox terriers, chow chows, rough collies and border collies, but when I saw shelties for the first time in 1950 at the Durham County Championship show I knew that was the breed for me. I have never regretted the decision, though I never dreamt at that time that it would lead to an international reputation judging in numerous countries, and providing me with lasting friendships around the world.

Shelties have gone through the popularity spiral and have now settled down and are established as one of the top breeds. They are not a get rich quick breed as there are so many points to get right in order to have an outstanding specimen, and also so many things which go wrong in the development stage. There are always more disappointments than successes and it requires patience and perseverance to succeed. As a result, many give up or turn to other easier breeds. Fortunately for the breed, there are a hard core of dedicated breeders who relish the challenge and apply themselves to the task with unfailing enthusiasm.

CHAPTER ONE

Starting in the Breed

WHETHER you require a puppy as a pet or as a show prospect, the best advice I can give is – be patient. The majority of beginners jump in with both feet and in most cases this leads to disappointment. If a show prospect is required, take your time. Visit as many championship and breed club shows as possible, prior to purchasing your dog. This will help you to decide on the type you prefer. Approach a reputable kennel and if in doubt, seek the advice of the breed club secretaries. Do not be satisfied with second best. There is an old saying in horse racing circles: 'You can't breed a Derby winner from a selling plater,' and the same is true of dogs. It is possible to produce a winner from poor breeding, what I call a lucky strike, but however much winning such a specimen may do, it rarely breeds on. If you think you are going to enjoy showing and breeding then I repeat, be patient and go for the best you can afford.

The ideal is to obtain a well bred young bitch and if she has done some winning, all the better. This type of bitch won't be easy to come by and she certainly won't be cheap, but it is the surest way to success. The next best thing is purchase a really good bitch puppy from a winner producing line. These days there are few large kennels who can hang on to all their puppies up to showable age, so obtaining a well bred puppy is not too difficult. Having obtained the puppy, the byword again is patience. Even if the puppy does not make championship show grade, do not discard it but mate it in due time to the most suitable dog, taking the advice of the breeder. It is also important to check the breeding records of the forebears of the puppy, particularly the bitches. Bitch puppies bred from good natural whelpers will tend to be the same. In our experience this runs in families and bitches from such lines have a strong mothering instinct and are absolute treasures to own.

The option to purchasing a young adult or a puppy is to obtain a bitch on breeding terms. I'm not particularly keen on this method but it has put some people on the road to success. On the other hand, it has caused much disappointment to both vendor and purchaser. The method can be applied with any bitch regardless of age, providing she is still young enough to breed from. Normally a much reduced price is paid, in some cases no money changes hands at all, and the terms vary from the pick of the first litter to first and third choice from the first two litters.

This can be a gentleman's agreement between friends. But in the long term it is much better to have a signed agreement setting out full details of the arrangement, taking account of any contingencies which may arise. A copy should be kept by the vendor and the purchaser. If all goes well, this is one way of obtaining a well bred bitch, particularly if the terms are not too severe.

However the pitfalls can be many and varied. For instance, the owner of the bitch will invariably wish to nominate the stud dog and this could be a dog situated at the other end of the country and entail expensive travel and hotel bills, apart from the stud fee. Secondly, the bitch can miss, which means the whole thing has to be undertaken all over again. If the terms are puppies from more than one litter, it can become a long drawn out affair before you own the bitch and before you can breed something worthwhile for yourself. Thirdly the bitch could be sterile, and how long does it take before this is finally established? The time span is two or three seasons at least. Fourthly, what if the bitch dies, from whatever cause? It can be a very complicated business and certainly not a situation to be entered into without considerable thought as to all the possible consequences.

CHAPTER TWO

Selecting a Puppy

I DON'T think it is too difficult even for a relative beginner to pick out the best puppy in a litter, whether the litter is good, bad or indifferent. But selecting a potential winner is a totally different kettle of fish. I find it much easier to see a litter for the first time at seven weeks, which is obviously not possible if you have bred the litter.

Go carefully over each pup, watch them move and then make your decision. This is what I did in the case of Champion Ellendale Prim of Plovern, Australian Champion Ellendale Etienne and Champion Marksman of Ellendale, to name but three. If you look at a litter from birth to seven or eight weeks, day in and day out, it can lead to much indecision. Puppies change so much at this stage and shelties in particular.

I always look for a balanced puppy which stands and moves well. I like a solid head with an evenly proportioned foreface and skull, well rounded muzzle with good underjaw, but not squared off at the nose as this usually draws out into an overlong foreface. Avoid fullness of the cheeks as this also indicates an overlong head. Ears should be medium sized and well placed, preferably a little heavy at this age as they invariably lift during the next two or three months.

The correct eye placement is there to be seen, even before the eyes open. The line of the eyelids should be obliquely set and not in a straight line. By seven or eight weeks the dark almond shaped eye should be obvious and that unique sheltie expression should be present. Even at this early age the skull should be flat and the stop well defined. Any with overlong forefaces, lack of stop and apple heads should be discarded. Straight or short upper arms, badly laid shoulders and high set tails are also obvious at an early age. These are very hereditary faults and should be avoided like the plague. A short neck is also obvious and is often allied to a straight upper arm and shoulder. Ultimate size is difficult to assess but we tend to discard the very heavy headed pups and the ones with over strong bone, big knuckles and large feet. Growth rate is fascinating and we have followed Dr Karin Riemann's theory and religiously weighed our pups and

A promising 10 week puppy. Note the flat skull, well defined stop, correct eye placement and strong underjaw.

kept records over several litters. We have found this to be the most reliable method of predicting ultimate size.

After examining the puppies at close quarters, stand away and watch them moving naturally at both ends and in profile. The bad movers can easily be spotted, and though fronts can sometimes tighten with maturity and exercise, weak back ends, cow hocks and elbows which are out, rarely improve with age. If the front movement looks wrong, check the angle of the upper arm and shoulder and the position of the elbows. If the hind action is suspect, check the thigh muscles and whether the hocks are straight when viewed from behind. The tail set is also important. Check the length of back, you don't want it too long or too short. Too long and the dog looks unbalanced, too short and it will look stuffy. It is not just coincidence that a short back so often goes with a short neck. A puppy of medium length with a good neck will always look elegant.

Make sure the puppy has good bone, nice oval feet and a good coat texture with plenty of undercoat and long guard hairs. In our experience good coats are bred for and no amount of vitamins and additives can make a dog carry a good coat. Temperament is also very important and again this is quite obvious from an early age. When you have seen a few litters from similar lines you will get a feel for the right type of puppy and this comes with experience, something that money can't buy. If you are uncertain ask for help, any genuine experienced breeder will be pleased to look at a litter. Once you lose your enthusiasm for looking at puppies, it is time to call it a day.

CHAPTER THREE

Predicting Size

by Dr Karin Riemann

*'Ideal height measured at the withers fourteen inches for bitches, fourteen and a
half inches for dogs. Anything more than one inch above these heights to be
considered a serious fault'.*

(The Standard, 1965).

*'Sheltie size is impossible to predict with certainty in a young puppy, which
accounts for many disappointments'.*

(O. Gwynne-Jones, 1958)

*'Another good thing to do is weigh the puppies every week till they are ten weeks
. . . I wish we had done it earlier but we only started a year or two ago and
already I can see it is going to be a most useful guide as to the puppies' eventual
size'.*

(F.M. Rogers, 1974)

AS these experts highlight, everybody involved in sheltie breeding knows
that size problems are still inherent in the breed and most of us have
experienced that these can occur in quite different dimensions and shapes.
Firstly, there is a certain moderate size variation in the sheltie, which is
more often extended towards the bigger sizes. Whether this is in accordance with the general trend in smaller breeds or originates in the fact that
the slightly oversized shelties are admittedly or unadmittedly preferred by
the breeders and exhibitors to those having ideal size, remains open to
discussion.

Secondly, there are additional size problems, which I should like to call
wrong sizes as the afflicted dogs are usually far apart from the sizes put
down in the Breed Standard. The first category of wrong sizes are the
miniature shelties, which can crop up quite frequently with some brood
bitches and sometimes afflict the whole litter. We have never experienced
these miniatures but should appreciate any information in order to get an
idea whether there is a dwarf factor or a hormone imbalance involved.

The second category of wrong sizes refers to the phenomenon that some lines tend to split in the way that they produce very small offspring, usually bitches, and rather big offspring, usually males, besides the ideal sizes. This was exactly what happened in our very first litter of five puppies. Two finished the ideal size, a dog fourteen and a half inches (37 cm), a bitch fourteen inches (35.5 cm) and another bitch of fourteen and a half inches. The third bitch puppy was the fattest during the first three weeks of puppyhood but stopped suddenly growing and finished at twelve inches (31 cm). The second dog in the litter was a big disappointment as when we saw him again at the age of eight months, not only was he a wrong size – eighteen and a half inches (47 cm) – he also seemed to be at variance with his sheltie ancestry in that he obviously displayed collie type. This was not, of course, the type of collie you are used to seeing in the show ring today.

We knew that shelties of the correct size may produce oversize shelties as this has long since been a problem, particularly when it comes to detecting the prospective grower in the litter. Strangely enough, there seems to no obvious indications that these growers may occasionally approach the enormous size of twenty inches (about 50 cm), even from mating where no oversized sheltie is in sight in the pedigree. The reason why some sheltie lines tend to split up this way seems as easy as complex.

Obviously this phenomenon still testifies for the collie crossings, which were done some fifteen male generations back in order to improve type. Subsequent to the collie cross the breeders did quite close line breeding to the collie ancestor which certainly has contributed to the genetical fixation of the collie heritage. The resurrection of those ancient collies in our sheltie litters suggests that the ideal sized generation between, were all carriers of the collie genes.

The different conditions and prerequisites for breeding and selling shelties in Germany as compared with Great Britain make it particularly essential to predict future size of a puppy, as oversize alongside dentition faults are the most frequent reasons for which shelties are banned from breeding. In addition, breeders in Germany tend to sell all their puppies at an early age but try to give the most promising ones to homes where future showing and breeding seems possible. Size prediction is either a gamble or the hard slog of some ten litters' apprenticeship in a country where the next breeder is about a hundred miles away and where no special breed clubs exist and where exhibiting of puppies is almost unknown.

Useful guides to estimate the final size of a puppy can be found in existing books on shetland sheepdogs but the breeders in question seem to need already a great deal of experience in order to give a more reliable prediction. Thus we felt fortunate when we discovered that the daily weight records of our first sheltie litter displayed the extremes as well as the ideals of sheltie sizes. This proved a valuable basis in our own attempt to recognise the eventual size of later born puppies at a comparatively early age. We even collected the weight records of several litters, including those of different breeders and sheltie lines and found that they all fitted into the respective growth pattern of our first puppies when comparing the period between five and eight weeks of the puppies' lives and their final sizes.

PRACTICAL PROCEDURE

All you need to try our method is a pair of scales enabling you to determine differences of a quarter of an ounce (about 7 grams) as well as the final weight of a ten week old puppy which may approach 10 pounds (4.5 kilograms). The puppies should be fed reasonably, there is no reason to change your usual rearing practice and starving a biggish puppy or over-feeding a small one will not influence the prospective size of the puppy. The puppies should be wormed according to the present knowledge of the parasites' reproductive cycle. It is also important to bear in mind that if there are any severe health problems before or while you are conducting the size prediction programme, the records can only be used with restrictions.

Dog breeders weigh their puppies in order to check their growth, the general health of the litter and the dam and to determine the time when additional feeding is needed. These were our aims when we started our weighing programme. But contrary to other breeders, we did not stop weighing at weaning time and these were the records that proved to be important for the prediction of size.

We discovered that weight at birth or at weaning time has no bearing at all on the eventual size of the puppy, no matter how fat or how tiny a puppy may be during his first weeks, it will not necessarily be the smallest or tallest in the litter. The best time for weighing is early morning, before the puppies get their first meal. It would be sufficient to weigh them twice a week but we found that daily weighing sets up a routine both for the breeder and the puppies and helps to avoid mistakes. Until the age of five weeks you can only speculate, but unless one or more puppies slow down their growth below 170 grams (six ounces) per week, there is no cause for concern. In fact, the puppies which end up being small are the first to show indications of this and by five weeks they are invariably the lightest puppies, with a weight below two pounds (900 grams). If you have such a puppy, in your litter and it is often a bitch it will probably stop growing at about twelve inches (30 cm).

By five weeks the tiny ones have revealed themselves, but there still remains the variants of those that are marginally too small, the ideal sizes, the too bigs and the giants, who don't care at all about the sizes asked for in the sheltie standard. These giants are the next to show their nature as they usually start to accelerate their growth rate by five weeks, putting on weight at the rate of about one pound (450 grams) during the following week. These puppies are usually males and there is little, if any hope, of them stopping at sixteen inches (40.6 cm). If they continue this growth rate over the next two weeks, they will attain a final size of between eighteen and twenty inches (45.5 and 51 cm).

By seven weeks you should know whether your litter contains any dwarfs or giants. If none of your puppies belong to these extremes, congratulations and good luck for the next week, as now the more precise calibration of the hopefuls begins. Incidentally, seven and eight weeks respectively are milestones for which sheltie breeders in both Great Britain and Germany have their size rules. Some British breeders like to have puppies not heavier than four pounds (1800 grams) by seven weeks, whereas Germans prefer the metric system and ask for puppies not heavier than two kilograms (4½ lbs) by eight weeks, when they expect the puppy to finish the correct size. However, these rules which are based on one

International Champion Riemann's Florian Pickenpack — Dr Riemann's favourite dog.

single weighing of the puppies, work as often as not. Big or first litters and lines in which puppies are usually small sizes at birth may stick to that rule, but single pups, small litters and lines with heavy puppies are generally well above this level and nevertheless finish a good size.

By contrast, the growth rate taken between five and eight weeks is found to reflect fairly well the later size, almost irrespective of the absolute weight at say five, seven or eight weeks. In my records I have three seven week old puppies with quite different absolute weights ranging from three and a half to four and half pounds and all have finished at fourteen and a half inches (37 cm). If the growth rate between five and eight weeks is compared it can be seen that these different puppies all put on weight of about two pounds (900 grams) during the last three weeks, which means that their average growth rate was close to eleven ounces (300 grams). This was in fact the most important result which I obtained from my studies.

Sheltie puppies who put on weight of about two pounds (900 grams) during the three weeks between the age of five and eight weeks will very probably finish the correct size later; bitches will finish close to fourteen inches (35.5 cm) and dogs close to fourteen and a half inches (37 cm).

The size prediction method may reduce the number of suspicious puppies or hidden growers in your litters, but there still remains the unpredictable puppy. These are the ones that show an increase of around 800 grams (1 lb 13 oz) during the crucial three week period. If you are lucky, they will just reach the ideals of the standard, if you are not, they will finish half an inch too small. On the other side of the scale, there is cause for concern with those which show three weeks growth rate of about 1100 grams (about 2½ lbs). The bitches may stop at fourteen and a half inches (37 cm) but they may also grow on to become fifteen and a half inches (39 cm) and the corresponding males may well be one inch above the level of the bitches. The remaining growth rate of 1000 grams usually results in slightly bigger shelties than the standard requires, bitches fourteen and a half inches and dogs fifteen inches, which many breeders and judges consider an acceptable size for a sheltie.

Many sheltie puppies go through stages from two months until they reach full size which may be bothering for the most optimistic breeder. Taking size records at the withers may cause additional concern, firstly as methodical deviations are very likely to occur and secondly, as the growth curve of an individual puppy is not that even. In fact, puppies finishing the same size can temporarily differ quite markedly in size. I experienced this recently when I reared two bitch puppies. One of them came from another kennel and from a different line but was only two days younger than my home bred puppy. I had predicted both their final sizes as four-

teen and a half inches but I could only feel sure about this when they were
eight months of age. Also, the later giants, which in our case often finished
at eighteen inches (46 cm) accelerated and retarded their growth at different times. This resulted in remarkable size differences between two and
twelve months, which we once experienced when we had three of these
fellows in one litter!

Final size also seems dependent on the time a sheltie stops growing.
Like size development, this varies greatly between lines as stated already
in the sheltie literature. There is a rule of thumb which at first sounds like
nonsense: the bigger a sheltie puppy is at seven months the more it will
continue to grow. That means that a tiny sheltie of about twelve inches
(30.5 cm) will have nearly reached its final size by about six months, the
ideal sized will usually not grow on considerably by seven months, whereas the sheltie who is already sixteen inches at seven months will very
probably grow one inch or more and will not stop growing until he is ten or
twelve months of age.

Whatever we might have thought or felt during later development of
our sheltie puppies, the early size prediction based on growth rate between
five and eight weeks of age proved to us the most reliable measure to assess
the prospective size.

SUMMARY
1. The weight of a puppy in the first three weeks of its life does not allow
   any conclusion on its later size. A single weighing from five weeks
   onwards gives only a very unreliable measure for predicting size. The
   most reliable prediction of size in shelties is believed to be the weight
   increase in the period between five and eight weeks.
2. The prospective sizes of the normally fed and wormed puppies can be
   assessed by weighing them daily and calculating the weekly and three-
   weekly growth rate. It may be helpful to draw a curve from these
   records.
3. The first size category you will discover is the smallest whose increase
   in weight is less than half a pound a week or less than one and a half
   pounds in the three week period.
4. The next to show their nature are the giants which increase as much or
   more than one pound per week or three pounds in the three week
   period – they will invariably grow above all limits.
5. Ideal sizes, put down in the sheltie standard will usually be obtained if
   puppies show a growth rate of about eleven ounces (300 grams) per
   week or two pounds (900 grams) during the crucial three weeks.

Troubleshooter of
Shemaur at 7 months.

Troubleshooter of
Shemaur at 5 years.

CHAPTER FOUR

Puppy Development

HOW nice it would be if all puppies grew up all of a piece. Some do and finish up among the best, while others go through all sorts of stages and still come back to being nice specimens. But what heartache it is when the puppy which was so promising at eight weeks suddenly lengthens in head, goes on the leg, loses it's attractive puppy fluff and looks an absolute horror. Pains in the gums when the second teeth are coming through cause the ears to go all over the place and you really do have an ugly duckling.

I was once talking with an experienced breeder, in my early days in the breed, and I was bemoaning the fact that my lovely puppy had gone on the leg. He replied: 'The trouble with you, young man, is you are like so many newcomers. You want your dogs to be kings before they have been princes'. Some pups, usually the really well bred ones, do become swans. But many fall by the wayside and this happens more with shelties than any other breed in which I have been involved.

I don't think any breed changes so much in the development stage as shelties and the two photographs of Troubleshooter of Shemaur highlight this. In fact, it is hard to believe it is the same dog. In the case of Shemaur-Travellin' Man the transition from youngster to adult was not quite so bad and in the case of Australian Champion Ellendale Etienne there was never an ugly stage, but the photos also illustrate the changes which will take place with maturity.

Shelties are usually great lasters, particularly the slow maturers. I much prefer a puppy who comes along slowly because these are the ones you will be showing well into their veteran years. I won my first challenge certificate with a puppy of seven months at the same time beating James G. Saunders for best of breed. James had made up a lovely mature bitch Helensdale Lena on the day and on reflection I don't think my puppy should have beaten her. I remember the judge's critique describing the puppy's early maturity and saying he had the perfect foreface. That really taught me a lesson because I've observed since that if a dog has the perfect foreface at that age, the skull often broadens early and the head finishes up

Shemaur Travellin'
Man at 10 months.

Shemaur Travellin'
Man at three years.

Australian champion Ellendale Etienne at 18 months.

Australian champion Ellendale Etienne at two and a half years.

Daleoak Damask Rosita (left) and Champion Daleoak Christmas Rose at nine weeks.

Daleoak Damask Rosita (left) and Champion Daleoak Christmas Rose as adults.

*Champion
Blenmerrow Oak
Apple.*

*Champion
Shelbrook
Whispering
Waves*

more like a working sheepdog. Also if you have the bone, body and coat of an adult dog at that early age, the dog almost inevitably coarsens just as my puppy did. I managed to win another challenge certificate with him but he never got his third and at two years old he looked like a rather coarse veteran.

I do love a laster, I've judged many championship shows and the breed has invariably turned up in strength, so that I can hardly envisage giving a puppy a challenge certificate because I always get so many good mature dogs. I think it's good for the breed when we have dogs who are not spectacular but steady winners with a long show career rather than the fly by nights. Two recent examples who typify what I mean by a laster are Champion Blenmerrow Oak Apple and Champion Shelbrook Whispering Waves, both of whom gained their titles at five years of age.

CHAPTER FIVE

Kennelling and Management

ONE of the best kennels I had was in North Yorkshire when my wife and I converted an old brick stable situated between the house and the garage. This was ideal, light and airy, and only exposed on two sides. We painted the interior walls with a white exterior paint, the concrete floor was sealed with a special colourless seal and, when dry, coated with 'liquid lino' which was easy to wash and looked smart. The door and windows were fitted with draught excluders. It was really snug and the dogs never had it so good.

At present, we have well constructed, insulated and lined wooden kennels with ample natural light, adequate ventilation and made as draught-proof as possible. Electric power is necessary for lighting, dryers and heaters. Over the years we have come to prefer thermostatic fan heaters to radiant heat lamps. They are economical to run and spread the heat quickly and can be stood safely on a shelf or fixed firmly to the wall, out of harm's way. It is essential that all electrical installations in kennels are done by a qualified electrician and all switches, points and wires should be high on the wall and well out of reach of inquisitive dogs.

The kennels are lined with polythene sheeting on top of which is one inch thick polystyrene insulation which is then covered with good quality plywood or plastic coated hardboard giving an easy-to-clean finish. The floors of the kennels are coated with a good quality wood stain, then after 48 hours drying period overcoated with yacht varnish. The roofs are covered with strong roofing felt and apart from fixing this with felt nails, wooden laths are also screwed on for extra hold against strong gales.

Three or four layers of newspaper are laid on the kennel floor at night or whenever the dogs are left. This can easily be lifted when soiled and burnt in the incinerator. Years ago fresh pine sawdust was a good absorbent for kennel floors, but nowadays most timber is impregnated with either preservatives or fire retardant solutions which give off vapours when wet and can be very irritating to the eyes and skin, so it is better not to risk it.

The kennels are placed on a concrete base and the surrounding runs laid

Kennel and run.

about three inches deep in road chippings, this drains well and is good for the feet. The good drainage enables the dogs to be out in all but the very worst weather and saves a lot of work washing and drying muddy dogs.

Shelties seem to prefer living as a group rather than separated in small kennels. In the main kennel, which is a building about ten feet by eight feet and six feet high at the centre, we usually have five to six adults – dogs and bitches – sleeping quite happily together. Each dog is provided with a robust wooden box on one inch bearers to provide an air gap. We use acrylic fabric – Vetbed – in the sleeping boxes, which is very cosy, easy to wash and dries quickly.

The exterior walls of the kennels are coated every year during the summer months with a good quality wood preserver such as Cuprinol, and the hinges and locks are kept well greased. Our kennels are always locked at night and when we are away from the house.

Our dogs are kennelled outside winter and summer but they are all given turns of being house dogs. It is essential that they are given plenty of time and training in the house, particularly as youngsters. We also like to let the old age pensioners end their days as house dogs, enjoying the

Shelties like living as a group.

Sheila and Maurice Baker exercising dogs.

comfort of a cosy fireside or pottering around in the garden as the fancy takes them.

Cleanliness they say is next to godliness, and certainly where dogs are concerned it is vital. Apart from the daily clearing out and tidying up of newspaper and bedding, it is essential to give floors, internal walls and sleeping boxes a weekly wash down with hot water and disinfectant. As we use newspaper which tends to shed its print on to the dogs, we find it necessary to change the Vetbeds at least twice a week and daily for puppies. It keeps the washing machine busy, but it's worth it to have clean dogs. Cleaning up the droppings in the runs and around the garden is a twice daily task, even more so with puppies. Disposing of used newspapers is a problem and we prefer to burn everything in the incinerator and then bag and dispose of the ash.

Exercise and feeding times are two very important aspects of daily management and are certainly highlights of the dogs' day. Providing the weather is suitable, we take the dogs as a pack into the woods first thing in the morning. This takes approximately one hour and it is anyone's guess how many miles the dogs cover during this time. But they all enjoy the freedom to run about as much as they like. When we return we put the dogs into their respective runs while we prepare the main meal. They always eat this with relish and then they are settled for the day. In the afternoons we give the dogs roadwork on a rota system. This is essential for the dogs which are being shown and the youngsters who are being trained.

CHAPTER SIX

Breeding

THERE is nothing more interesting or absorbing than the first litter you breed. Hopefully your well bred puppy has made up into a nice specimen and now the next step is to improve on her with the next generation. There is no laid down formula for selecting a stud dog that will guarantee the desired result, but there are some important guidelines which shorten the odds.

Do not select a stud dog just because you are attracted to him in the show ring. If you really like him, then take a look at his sire which might be a better choice. A dog that has consistently produced winners is a better prospect than a dog, however good looking, who has produced nothing. So don't allow yourself to be a guinea pig.

Study the English Shetland Sheepdog Club Charts and shortlist three or four dogs from the same family and line as your bitch. Check their stud records from the charts or with the help of the owners for there is no point in using a dog that has thrown nothing of quality. If the stud records of your selected sires are fairly even, then look at their physical and mental qualities and take the one who excels in the points where your bitch fails. Whatever you do, don't use a dog with the same faults as your bitch or you will simply be doubling up on these. If you purchased your bitch from a kennel of longstanding reputation, then the breeder could give invaluable advice as he will know most of the virtues and faults of the dogs and bitches in the pedigree.

An experienced stud dog is really essential for a maiden bitch because he will do the business with a minimum of fuss and not be put off by a coy young maiden. Watch your bitch carefully and when she is nearing the six months period from the previous season examine her every day. It is most important that you know the exact day she comes into season, and advise the stud dog owner immediately as the best dogs do get booked up quickly. In our experience it is better to mate a maiden bitch later rather than earlier in the season so that you benefit from full ovulation. Maiden bitches are rarely ready before the fourteenth day and more often not until the fifteenth or sixteenth day from the start of the season. The biggest error made by most first time breeders is mating the bitch too early. It seems to be over anxiety to get the job done or a fear of being too late.

If you are not sure about the right day, seek advice from an experienced breeder. The ideal time is usually the day the bitch stops showing colour at which time the swollen vulva will have softened to permit easy penetration. There is nothing more galling for the stud dog owner than to have a bitch presented for mating on the wrong day. The bitch will not be receptive and this will be frustrating for all concerned, not least the stud dog. On the correct day the bitch will stand firm, move her tail to one side and generally play up to the dog. With a maiden bitch there may be some resistance even on the correct day, and in this case a mild sedative will help to relax her. Also with a maiden there is always the possibility of a stricture which is simply a very thin membrane usually two inches or so from the entrance to the vulva. The experienced stud dog owner will always examine a maiden bitch using a well greased finger and will simply and painlessly break down a stricture if one is present.

Do make sure your bitch is groomed and clean when you visit the dog. It is most discourteous to take an unkempt, grubby bitch to be mated. The responsible stud dog owner you can be sure will have his dog looking immaculate when you visit, it gives a good impression, and he will want you to see the dog at his best. The stud fee is payable at the time of mating. Remember you are paying for the service – it is not a guarantee of a litter, though there is usually a gentleman's agreement of a free mating in the event of a bitch missing.

You will need a Kennel Club form signed by the stud dog owner to confirm the mating and to register the litter and this is usually supplied by the stud dog owner together with a stud receipt showing the date the bitch is due to whelp and a copy of the stud dog's pedigree, if this has not been sent to you earlier.

However good the stud dog you choose, it's as well to remember that all puppies have a mother, and she has a big influence on the litter. Invariably when people see a nice puppy at a show they turn up the catalogue and check on the sire, the poor mum is rarely considered. But of course it's always the sire who gets the credit if the pups are good, and inevitably the blame if the pups are of poor quality, regardless of the quality of the dam. I always remember dear old Miss Grey of the Ladypark collies when she had International Champion Lochinvar of Ladypark at stud saying to me: 'You know they bring bitches like rocking horses to this dog and expect him to put everything right!'

CHAPTER SEVEN

The Stud Dog

WE have had a team of champion stud dogs for some years, so we have experienced most of the ups and downs of stud work. Big bitches, small bitches, early bitches, late bitches, dirty bitches and occasionally, very occasionally, a disinterested dog. But through it all, we have managed to retain a sense of humour.

Apart from maidens, the most difficult bitches to mate are pets who are not used to mixing with other dogs. Kennel bitches who live in groups are generally more amenable. Strangely enough, bitches who are sent to us and stay a few days are usually the least bother. When they are away from their owners, they seem to be on their best behaviour. We do not subscribe to the theory that a dog must be introduced to stud work before it is a year old, in order to be successful. Many of the best and efficient stud dogs have started in their second year. It is a mistake to try and force a dog to mate a bitch before he is ready. They all mature sexually at different ages and it is far better to wait until the dog will willingly and enthusiastically mate a bitch, rather than try to make him perform because you think he has reached an age when he should start his stud career. This will only lead to frayed tempers, frustration and a lot of wasted time, and possibly a dog who may never make a successful stud dog.

The ideal introduction for a maiden dog is a really experienced bitch with a good breeding record, a slim figure and preferably the correct size. We have had some like this, who will virtually mate the dog and they are invaluable. It is always advisable to undertake the mating in a quiet room where there are no distractions from other people, dogs, telephones or television. Make sure that both dog and bitch are standing on a non-slip surface, such as a fibre mat or similar. Often with a first time mating the dog will be keenly interested and willing to mount the bitch when she is free, but show disinclination when her head is held. Do not be tempted to let him do it his way or to leave the dog alone with the bitch. It is fatal. He must be made to realise that the bitch has to be held.

Always examine the bitch, make sure she is ready and vaseline the vulva before the dog is introduced. The owner must hold the bitch's head firmly so that you can put one hand underneath the bitch and hold the vulva towards the dog with two fingers projecting to form a guide for the dog to strike. Hold the bitch's tail to one side with the other hand. If the bitch is brought at the right time, she will be giving off a strong scent which will encourage the dog and hopefully she will thrust her rear end towards him inviting him to mount.

Don't give up if the dog mounts the bitch several times and gets off again quickly. At least he has the right idea and if you practice patience and perseverance he will eventually get there. When this happens and the dog starts to work vigorously, let go of the bitch's tail and slowly and gently put your arm round the back of the dog to steady him. Once the dog has finished working and you can feel with the hand under the bitch that they are tied, don't be in too much of a hurry to turn him. Just let him relax on the bitch's back for a few moments and tell him what a clever boy he is. Then gently lift his forelegs from the bitch and place them at her side, then ease his outside back leg over the bitch so that they are standing back to back, all the time praising the dog. For the duration of the tie, sit quietly next to the pair holding their tails together in one hand just in case either should try to pull away too soon. After ten to twenty minutes or so they will naturally part — again praise is due for a good job well done.

Before letting the dog join the rest of his kennelmates, sponge him down gently underneath with a mild antiseptic solution, then let him rest on his laurels. It is advisable to have a second mating after 48 hours if the dog is a maiden, though not always necessary as many young dogs produce litters from a first single mating. All dogs are different in their technique. Some want to turn quickly and some hang on for grim death. It is the same with the tie. It's surprising how this varies with different dogs but after a few matings you get to know your dog's idiosyncracies. It is reassuring to have a tie of at least ten minutes but this is not strictly necessary as the sperm passes into the bitch in the first minute or so. During the rest of the tie the dog is simply pumping a clear fluid into the bitch which serves to wash the sperm up through the cervix. Some of this liquid often runs out of the bitch immediately after mating. This is quite natural and nothing to be concerned about, she will have lost none of the fertile sperm.

Always praise the dog and the bitch when the job has been done correctly and never ever lose your temper. Patience is a virtue where stud work is concerned. Also if you value your stud dog's reputation don't let him mate any bitch that comes along, regardless of breeding and type. When you advertise your dog's at stud to approved bitches, let it mean just that.

CHAPTER EIGHT

Whelping and Weaning

ONCE your bitch has been mated, keep her confined to your own property and her normal exercising areas and walks. I have never shown a bitch after she has been mated, there are enough problems without exposing her to the obvious risk of infection at a general championship show, or indeed any show.

We do not change the feed or give additives too early in the pregnancy as it is all too easy for the bitch to put on unwanted weight which is no help at all at whelping time. We believe in plain nutritious food, a constant supply of fresh water and normal exercise. We also believe in regular grooming throughout the pregnancy. It keeps the bitch feeling good and as we always chat to her during the grooming it keeps her happy which is most important. We give an extra milk and cereal meal from the fifth or sixth week onwards, depending on whether we think the bitch is heavily in whelp, and also increase the amount of meat in the main meal. Towards the end, it is advisable to divide the main meat meal into two small meals as a bitch heavily in whelp hasn't the stomach room to accept a large meal all at once.

At least a week before whelping we bring the bitch into the house and introduce her to the whelping quarters. At this time it is advisable to take her temperature night and morning. At a week before whelping it will be around a hundred degrees Fahrenheit, then a couple of days before the puppies are born it will slowly start to drop until it reaches human level – around ninety eight degrees Fahrenheit. When this happens you know the puppies are due within twelve hours and this is the time to start watching for the first signs of labour.

We whelp our bitches in ample sized open wooden boxes lined with plenty of clean newspaper so that the bitch can have the satisfaction of ripping this up to make her nest. We have a supply of clean newspaper, towels and a bowl of hot water with antiseptic solution available. We also make sure we have some kitchen roll which can be handy for getting a grip on a slippery wet whelp which is having difficulty getting into the world, perhaps a breech birth. It is also useful to have sterilised scissors ready just in case the bitch doesn't sever the cord herself and also a small box containing a hot water bottle covered with a piece of acrylic fibre material in case you need to put a newly born pup to one side while dealing with the next one. Although, in our experience bitches don't like their babies separated and are usually washing one while the next one is arriving. At this time it is very important to keep the temperature of the room quite high, even if it is uncomfortable for the bitch as it is important that the puppies are dried and warmed quickly. Once they are all warm, dry and settled, the temperature can be adjusted to suit the bitch.

Prior to parturition the bitch will become very restless, often pacing about the room, panting and licking the vulva. She will probably ask to go outside to spend a penny frequently, and when she does so keep an eye on her as it has been known for bitches to drop their first born literally under the gooseberry bush!

Actual labour commences when the bitch starts straining and a note of this time should be taken as following this the first puppy should arrive within about an a hour and a half. If nothing has happened after this time it is advisable to seek professional advice as there may be complications and too long a delay in treatment could be disastrous. When straining becomes intense the water bag appears which looks rather like a small balloon filled with dark liquid. This makes way for the puppy and usually after two or three hard pushes the puppy appears. The bitch will immediately start cleaning up operations, licking up the liquid from the bag and hopefully remove the membrane which covers the puppy and bite the cord, which is much better than cutting it. If she shows no inclination to do this quickly open the bag yourself and present the cord to the bitch to sever. If you have to cut the cord yourself, do it with sterilised blunt rather than sharp scissors as this will minimise the bleeding. Cut the cord near to the placenta leaving a long cord on the puppy which the bitch will almost certainly trim to the correct length. We always try to discreetly dispose of the placenta rather than let the bitch follow her natural instinct to eat it. Bitches who consume the afterbirths tend to get rather nasty black diarrhoea, which we prefer to avoid. Obviously in the wild state it was necessary for it to be eaten to sustain the bitch for the first hours of her confinement, however in these days of modern nutritious feeding this is unnecessary and we prefer to give the bitch a light meal of scrambled egg or chicken when she feels ready to accept it.

Shelties are usually easy whelpers and good mothers but there is the occasional difficult one which disproves the rule. We always stay with our bitches, whatever time they start whelping and however inconvenient. We are sure it gives confidence and settles the bitch and sometimes, particularly with a maiden, they do not always get the first puppy out of the bag quickly enough and it can get waterlogged and suffocate, so it is essential to be in attendance. It is an experience we don't like to miss; however many litters you have brought into the world, it is still exciting to watch the miracle of birth.

It is amazing how quickly even a maiden bitch will learn to clean up and stimulate the puppies. Some bitches pass quite a lot of water with each puppy and so the first arrivals are continually getting wet with each new arrival. It is therefore useful to have a warm towel ready to rub them down and also a supply of newspaper handy to cover and absorb the puddles in the box. It is best not to disturb the bitch by continually changing the paper, but to add dry layers until she has completely finished and settled down with her new family. Then simply dispose of all the soiled newspaper, line the box with a thick layer of fresh paper and cover this with a clean acrylic fibre blanket and leave mother in peace to enjoy her babies.

It is advisable to keep an eye on them for the first few hours to make sure all the puppies are suckling strongly. It is also necessary to comb out the bitch's tail and petticoats so that there are no knots for the new born puppies to get entangled in. Once you are sure all is well, do not fuss. Just leave her to get on with things, allow no unnecessary distractions and never allow casual visitors in to disturb her. The bitch will probably not want solid food for some hours after the birth, but a drink of diluted milk perhaps with an egg beaten into it will probably be appreciated. Always have a bowl of water right next to her box. The bitch needs plenty to drink to ensure a good milk supply and unless the water is near at hand she won't want to leave her puppies to go and drink.

For the first three weeks after birth the bitch will require extra nourishment, especially if she has a good sized litter. We give her three meals a day, two of meat and biscuit and one cereal and milk feed. These feeds can gradually be reduced during the weaning period so that by the time the puppies are five weeks old the bitch is back to her normal one meal a day feeding routine.

Whether you are keeping the bitch in the house or in a kennel, make sure that the temperature is somewhere around seventy degrees Fahrenheit for at least two weeks. Keep a thermometer in the room and check it regularly. Warmth and cleanliness are absolutely essential if your litter is to thrive and grow properly. We have used infra-red lamps and these must be kept at a reasonable height from the box so as not to overheat the bitch. But some bitches object to having constant heat hanging over them and so we now prefer to use thermostatically controlled fan heaters fixed to the wall or stood on a shelf positioned close to the whelping box. It saves a lot of worry if, for instance, there is a sudden drop in temperature during the night, you have peace of mind knowing the whelping room will be kept at a steady temperature.

Check the bitch's milk glands to ensure all teats are being suckled and if any appear hard and lumpy, draw off some milk by hand until the teats are small enough to fit into the puppies' mouths. Then encourage the pups to use these teats by holding a pup close to the teat. Do remember to trim the puppies' nails at least once a week, otherwise the mother's tummy will become sore and feeding will be an uncomfortable experience for her.

We advise the removal of dew claws. An adult dog can bleed profusely when one is accidentally torn. We remove them with a pair of fairly blunt sterilised scissors when the puppies are three days old. It is a very simple operation and most do not even bleed. But if some bleeding does occur this is easily stopped with the application of a silver nitrate pencil which can be bought from any chemist or with a few crystals of permanganate of potash.

Weaning should be commenced when the puppies are three weeks old and shelties are rarely difficult in this respect. We start by introducing a midday meal of crumbled Weetabix soaked with diluted evaporated milk and sweetened with a little honey. It should be of a thick creamy consistency, and once the puppies' noses are gently pushed towards the food they soon start lapping. Two days later, an evening meal of Weetabix is offered and then between three and a half and four weeks we introduce cooked finely minced meat and gravy as a morning feed, again mixed with crushed Weetabix. During this time the bitch should be taken away from the pups for increasing periods of time, especially just before feeding time. Then by the time the pups are five weeks old, she should only be with them at night or if you feel she is ready, she can be taken away from them altogether. She will then be happy with quick, occasional visits to check that all is well. We usually find young bitches with their first litter tend to lose interest a little during the weaning period. But as they get older and more experienced, their maternal instinct seems to grow and they are even prepared to help out with litters other than their own.

At five weeks of age our puppies have the following diet:
Morning: Minced meat (beef or chicken) with crushed Weetabix or soaked puppy meal.
Midday: A drink of milk.
Teatime: Scrambled egg with crumbled wholemeal bread or tinned creamed rice pudding.

Bedtime: Weetabix and milk or porridge

At seven weeks we cut out the midday drink of milk so that when the puppies go to their new homes they are on three meals a day. Often when a puppy leaves the competition of his littermates, his appetite slackens and he appreciates his food more when only fed three times a day.

WORMING

We dose the puppies for roundworms at five weeks, providing the pups are of normal size and healthy. There are many safe and efficient worming remedies on the market and we use piperazine. But it is always best to be guided by your vet. We repeat the dose after ten days whether or not the puppies have passed worms from the first dose. It is also essential to worm the mother at the same time as she has been cleaning up after the puppies and so will have picked up any infection present.

INOCULATIONS

Inoculation is absolutely essential these days with so many people keeping dogs and it is even more vital if you are a regular showgoer. Again, there are many brands of vaccine available and it is wise to consult your vet about the right age for the first injection, as this varies with the type of vaccine. Do make sure that the full course of vaccination has been carried out against distemper, hepatitis, leptospirosis and parvovirus and that the puppy is kept in for the necessary quarantine period, usually about two weeks, following vaccination.

HAND REARING

If the bitch loses her milk supply then a foster mother is the ideal substitute, particularly if it is another sheltie. But foster mothers are never easy to find at the critical time. The alternative, but not to be undertaken lightly, is to attempt to hand-rear the whelps. It can be done successfully but needs absolute dedication. It is a demanding, tiring, thankless and often fruitless task.

The puppies must be fed every two hours day and night and for this a special small sized bottle and teat is needed. These are readily available at most good pet shops. But it is a good idea to have one or two of these bottles in the cupboard in case of emergencies, as these always seem to occur during the night or on a Sunday! On the odd occasion we have had to hand rear we have found that evaporated milk diluted with an equal amount of boiled water and sweetened with a little honey is the best. The puppies seem to accept and digest it much more easily than cows milk. Warm water and glucose or warm water and honey is also easily taken if a pup is weak and this prevents dehydration.

It is also important to observe the puppies' motions and look out for the first signs of diarrhoea which can pull a young puppy down so quickly. Even when the puppies are suckling normally, watch out for wet bottoms and sore anal glands. This is a sure sign that the bitch is having to clean the puppies too frequently because of loose motions. If this is the case, then observe the bitch and if she is also loose she may have an infection which is being passed on to the puppies. Immediate action is called for. An antibiotic for the bitch and possibly Lectade for the puppies which gives them all they require in the way of vitamins and prevents dehydration which can occur so quickly in tiny puppies. Lectade is a rehydration preparation only available from the vet, whose advice should of course be sought immediately symptoms of diarrhoea occur.

Strict attention should be paid to hygiene. The anus should be dried and cleaned at regular intervals and smeared with an antiseptic cream which will relieve the soreness and soon bring things back to normal. These problems apart, it is highly rewarding to care for young puppies and when you finish up with a strong healthy litter you know that all your efforts have been worthwhile.

CHAPTER NINE

Rearing and Training

WHEN a puppy is separated from his littermates he will miss the company and the competition, particularly at feeding time when he may go off his feed for a little while. The solution is to reduce the quantity of food slightly and vary the diet to keep it interesting and stick to the same meal times.

One golden rule at this time, or at any time for that matter, is never ever leave food lying around, particularly overnight in the hope that the puppy will eat at his leisure. If you do, the puppy will pick at the food, just taking the edge off his appetite and never get hungry enough to enjoy a good meal. If a meal is not eaten at the proper time, remove it and give nothing until the next feeding time. Never give titbits between meals and always have a supply of fresh water available.

Most breeders will give a diet sheet showing exactly how the puppy has been fed and it is a mistake to change this drastically when he changes homes. Try to keep the diet as near as possible to what the puppy is used to. If you wish to introduce a different diet, do so gradually and don't start the change until the puppy has settled down with you. From about seven weeks onwards we feed three meals a day, as outlined in the chapter on Whelping and Weaning. We prefer to use diluted evaporated milk or goats milk with the cereal rather than cows milk or powdered milk. We reduce to two meals a day at six months by cutting out the afternoon feed and then at about nine months we go on to one good meal a day of meat and mixer or wholemeal puppy meal. We find that even the adult shelties prefer the smaller puppy meal or mixer to large chunks of biscuit meal. The adults also have a few Shapes or Biscrock biscuits at bedtime.

I am a great believer in starting training as early as possible and once I have selected my puppy, the first thing I do is get him used to standing naturally and confidently on the grooming table. I always place a piece of carpet on the table to give a good footing. I set the puppy on the table four square and coax him to stand in position, talking all the time to encourage him. Some puppies take to it easily, others can be more difficult. But with patience, it is surprising how quickly they will stand as you want them to. With a soft to medium bristle brush I then brush gently the wrong way from tail to head, still talking to give the puppy confidence. It is essential to do this as often as possible, practice makes perfect. Once the puppy is standing steadily, it is time to get down to the serious business of grooming as this is the routine he must get used to and accept if you are going to present him to the best advantage. Using a fine plant spray filled with rain water, spray the coat all over avoiding the ears, then towel lightly. Brush quite vigorously from tail to head until the coat is dry then brush lightly from head to tail. Dust the white parts with talcum powder, then brush out and the puppy will look a picture.

Use a fine toothcomb to tease out the soft hair around the ears, leg fringes and any tangles under the tail. It is also essential at this time to get the puppy used to having his feet and hocks trimmed and his nails clipped. During these grooming sessions take the opportunity to open the mouth and examine the teeth. If this is done regularly, you will never have any problems on the judging table. When you have doggy friends visiting, ask them to go over the puppy on the table and look at the mouth. This gets puppies used to being handled by strangers.

Lead training can sometimes be difficult and at other times easy, depending on the temperament of the puppy. My wife and I have differing opinions on this. I prefer to start at about eight to ten weeks but Sheila waits until the puppy is four to five months. Both methods seem equally successful. The main thing is to encourage the puppy, never use force, talk to him and use some tasty titbits and he will soon get the idea. The object is to make walking on the lead an enjoyable activity and not a clash of wills. Strangely enough, the noisy jumping jackasses are usually the first to come round. It's the stubborn, sit down, won't move, types that take the time. But all succumb with patience, sympathetic handling and an even temper.

CHAPTER TEN

Selling a Puppy

THE time will come when you will have puppies for sale and as a responsible breeder you will be concerned about their future and careful about who you sell the pups to. Apart from advertising in Dog World and Our Dogs, you will find that most of the breed clubs run a puppy register and usually have a good number of enquiries channelled through them from genuine would-be owners. For this service a very small sum is charged which goes towards the breed club funds.

Again, as a responsible breeder, do things properly and be proud of your after sales service. It is surprising how many repeat orders come from people who appreciate your interest and advice following the sale, even after many years. Always question the potential buyer to make sure they have given sufficient thought to owning a dog. Ask if they have owned a dog before and have they suitable premises. Don't be put off automatically by a couple who both work – we have had such buyers who have made perfect owners, sometimes even taking a puppy to work or being able to pop home a couple of times during working hours. But do make sure they realise their responsibilities and can make adequate arrangements for the puppy's welfare.

Once satisfied, you will need to provide them with a copy of the pedigree, the Kennel Club registration/transfer form, diet sheet and some advice on grooming, training and inoculations. We always insist on new owners coming to collect the puppy as we do not think an unaccompanied journey suitable for a young puppy of eight weeks or so. But if you do need to despatch a puppy by rail, you will need a suitable travelling box. Check with the station beforehand to make sure which trains will take livestock and arrive at least half an hour early in order to give the station staff time to weigh and label the box correctly. Make sure the box carries your name and telephone number as well as the particulars of the new owner, take the box on to the train along with the porter and try to have a word with the guard. In these days of high speed inter-city services, no journey should be so long as to warrant feeding en route, so long as they are going from one

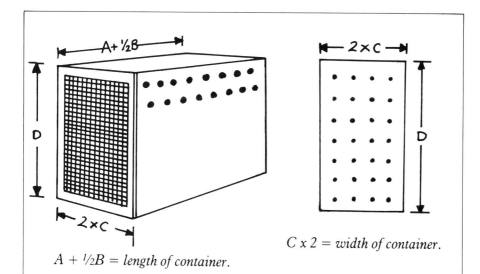

A + ¹/₂B = length of container.

C x 2 = width of container.

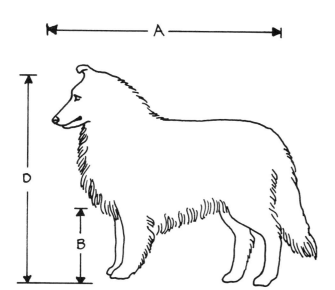

A = length from nose to root of tail.
B = Height from ground to elbow joint.
C = Width across shoulders.
D = Height of container — Height of dog in standing position.

These measurements must be verified by a veterinary surgeon and appear on the health certificate.

Travelling container

mainline station to another, hopefully with no change of trains on the journey.

As you progress in the breed, you may be asked to export a dog. The export and traffic of dogs from one country to another is subject to a great deal of control and regulation and rightly so. Documentation in connection with this can be quite complex so it is wise to make arrangements some weeks in advance of the departure date.

The first step is to approach your veterinary surgeon who should have a copy of all the Ministry of Agriculture and veterinary regulations for entry into each particular country. These will state what inoculations are needed and the blood tests and health certificates which are necessary. In this respect, the matter of timing is most important as countries have different regulations on the number of days a blood test or inoculation is valid before travel.

Most exports nowadays are by air and the type of container is most important. There are strict regulations as to size and construction and if not complied with the airline can refuse to carry the dog. Containers may be made of wood, fibreglass, metal, rigid plastic or wickerwork, though the latter is only acceptable for dogs weighing up to three kilos (7 lbs). Containers must be smooth on the inside so the dog cannot damage itself. One end must have bars or strong weld mesh, not wire netting, from top to bottom. The opposite end must also have ventilation from top to bottom, as must the upper third of each side. Holes should be approximately two centimetres or three-quarters of an inch in diameter. The access can be either a sliding or hinged door which must be capable of being secured or padlocked from the outside. The container must also be paw and nose proof. The size of the box is also important. The dog should be able to stand in a normal upright position, turn around and sit down naturally. In accordance with International Air Transport Association Live Animal Regulations all travelling boxes must display mandatory 'This Way Up' labels and green 'Live Animal' labels.

If you wish, you can provide your own box. However, there are a number of freight companies with offices at the cargo department of most airports, and usually at least one of these deals with livestock. They are very helpful and will give you a quote for providing a full service, including obtaining a suitable box, if you let them know the date of travel, size and weight of the dog and destination. This will be done over the telephone, then all you need to do is get the necessary veterinary papers and deliver the dog to the freight company at the specified time.

If possible the dog should be introduced to the container a few days before travel. This will help him to accept the travelling conditions more readily. A familiar blanket, rug or plaything will also make the container more acceptable. The outside of the container must be clearly marked with the address to which the dog is travelling and the dog's pet name. The use of tranquillisers or sedation is neither necessary nor recommended because if a drowsy animal wakes up in mid flight, his behaviour can be unpredictable. It is also necessary to have a label on the box stating when the dog was last fed and watered.

CHAPTER ELEVEN

The Standard

THE Kennel Club have recently reviewed all the breed standards including that of the shetland sheepdog which has been modified and reduced. But I believe the original standard is far more descriptive. It has served the breed very well over the years and it is still the one that I prefer.

Characteristics: To enable the shetland sheepdog to fulfil its natural bent for sheepdog work, its physical structure should be on the lines of strength and activity, free from cloddiness and without any trace of coarseness. Although the desired type is similar to that of the rough collie there are

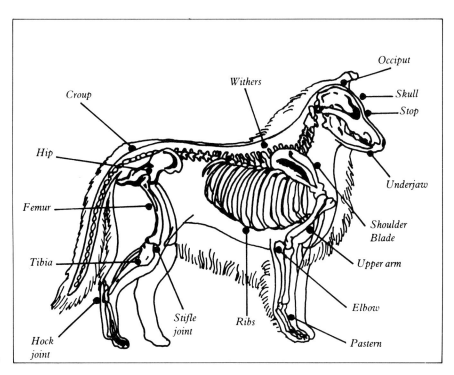

*Anatomy of the
Shetland Sheepdog.*

marked differences that must be noted. The expression, being one of the most marked characteristics of the breed, is obtained by the perfect balance and combination of skull and foreface, size, shape, colour and placement of eyes, correct position and carriage of ears, all harmoniously blended to produce that almost indefinable look of sweet, alert, gentle intelligence. The shetland sheepdog should show affection and response to his owner, he may show reserve to strangers but not to the point of nervousness.

General Appearance: The shetland sheepdog should instantly appeal as a dog of great beauty, intelligence and alertness. Action lithe and graceful with speed and jumping power, great for its size. The outline should be symmetrical so that no part appears out of proportion to the whole. An abundance of coat, mane and frill, with shapeliness of head and sweetness of expression all combine to present the ideal shetland sheepdog that will inspire and secure admiration.

Head and Skull: The head should be refined and its shape when viewed from the top or side is a long blunt wedge tapering from ear to nose. The width of skull necessarily depends upon the combined length of skull and muzzle and the whole must be considered in connection with the size of the dog. The skull should be flat, moderately wide between the ears, showing no prominence of the occipital bone. Cheeks should be flat and merge smoothly into a well rounded muzzle. Skull and muzzle to be of equal length, central point to be the inner corner of the eye. In profile the topline of the skull should be parallel to the topline of the muzzle, but on a higher plane due to a slight but definite stop. The jaws should be clean and strong and with a well developed underjaw. Lips should be tight. Teeth should be sound and level, with an evenly spaced scissor bite.

Eyes: A very important feature giving expression to the dog. They should be of medium size obliquely set and of almond shape. Colour dark brown except in the case of merles, where blue is permissible.

Ears: Should be small and moderately wide at the base, placed fairly close together on the top of the skull. When in repose they should be thrown back, but when on the alert brought forward and carried semi-erect with tips dropping forward.

Neck: The neck should be muscular, well arched and of sufficient length to carry the head proudly.

*Correct head showing parallel planes,
oblique eyes, well developed underjaw.*

*"Old fashioned" head, short,
stop too deep, head too deep through.*

*"Dish faced", bumpy skull,
lack of underjaw.*

*Lack of stop, jaws receding too
quickly under nose, small eye
giving hard expression*

*Receding skull, weak
underjaw.*

"Roman nose", stop not clearly defined.

This head typifies the requirements of the standard. Note the well developed underjaw and tight lips, also shape and placement of eye.

Body and Quarters: From the withers the shoulder blade should slope at a 45 degree angle, forward and downward to the shoulder joint. At the withers they are separated only by the vertebrae, but they must slope outwards to accommodate the desired spring of ribs. The upper arm should join the shoulder blade as close to a right angle as possible. The elbow joint should be equi-distant from the ground and the withers. The forelegs should be straight when viewed from the front, muscular and clean, with strong bone. The pasterns should be strong and flexible. The body is slightly longer from the withers to the root of the tail than the height at the withers, but most of the length is due to the proper angulation of the shoulder and hind quarters.

The chest should be deep reaching to the point of the elbow. The ribs should be well sprung but tapering at their lower level to allow free play of the forelegs and shoulders. The back should be level with a graceful sweep over the loins and the croup should slope gradually to the rear. The thigh should be broad and muscular, the thigh bones to be set into the pelvis at right angles, corresponding to the angle of the shoulder blade. The stifle joint where the femur bone joins the tibia bone must have a distinct angle, hock joint to be clean cut, angular and well let down with strong bone. The hock must be straight when viewed from behind.

Tail: Set on low, tapering bone must reach at least to the hock joint, with abundant hair and slight upward sweep, raised when the dog is moving but never over the level of the back.

Feet: Oval in shape, soles well padded, toes arched and close together.

Gait: The action of the shetland sheepdog should denote speed and smoothness. There should be no pacing, plaiting, rolling or stiff stilted up and down movement.

Coat: Must be double, the outer coat of long hair of harsh texture and straight, the under coat soft (resembling fur) short and close. The mane and frill should be very abundant and forelegs well feathered. Hind legs above the hocks profusely covered with hair, but below the hocks fairly smooth. The mask or face smooth. What are commonly known as smooth coated specimens are barred.

Colour: Tri colours should be an intense black on body with no signs of ticking, rich tan markings on a tri colour to be preferred. Sables may be clear or shaded, any colour from gold to deep mahogany but in its shade the colour should be rich in tones. Wolf sable and grey colours are undesirable. Blue merles, clear silvery blue is desired, splashed and marbled with black. Rich tan markings to be preferred, but the absence not to be counted as a fault. Heavy black markings, slate coloured or rusty tinge in either top or undercoat is highly undesirable. General effect should be blue.

   White markings may be shown in the blaze, collar, chest frill, legs, stifle and tip of tail. All or some tan markings may be shown on eyebrows, cheeks, legs, stifles and under tail. All or some of the white markings are to be preferred whatever the colour of the dog, but the absence of these markings shall not be considered a fault. Black and white and black and tan are also recognised colours. Over markings of patches of white on the body are highly undesirable. The nose must be black whatever the colour of the dog.

Size: Ideal height measured at the withers: 14 ins for bitches, 14½ ins for dogs. Anything more than one inch above these heights to be considered a serious fault.

Faults: Domed or receding skull, lack of stop, large drooping or pricked ears, over-developed cheeks, weak jaw, snipy muzzle, not full complement of teeth, crooked forelegs, cow hocks, tail kinked, short or carried over the back, white or white colour predominating. Pink or flesh coloured nose, blue eyes in any other colour than merles. Nervousness. Full or light eye. Under or overshot mouth.

Shetland Sheepdog
Champion
Forestland Tassel.

Rough collie
Champion Sandiacre
Stripper.

CHAPTER TWELVE

The Rough Collie and the Sheltie

IF you talk to the man in the street he will invariably refer to the sheltie as a miniature collie which, of course, it isn't. Nevertheless, what we owe to the first collie crosses for putting the quality into our breed is incalculable.

The old breeders were anything but stupid when as the breed was developing they drew up the original standard to read:

'General Appearance: is that of the rough collie in miniature (collie type must be adhered to).'

Later the English Shetland Sheepdog Club, the Northern Counties Shetland Sheepdog Club and the Scottish Shetland Sheepdog Club jointly agreed to amend this to read: 'Although the desired type is similar to the rough collie, there are marked differences that must be noted.' This was approved by the Kennel Club at its meeting of June 28, 1965.

The first and most obvious of these differences is of course size where the respective requirements are:

Rough collie: Dogs — twenty-two to twenty-four inches at shoulder; Bitches-twenty to twenty-two inches at shoulder.

Shetland sheepdog: Dogs — ideal height fourteen-and-a-half inches with one inch allowance above and below. Bitches — ideal height fourteen inches with one inch allowance above and below.

I do feel that you have to own and breed both breeds to fully appreciate the differences. My first collie Danvis Diana was a complete lady in every respect. She was quiet, unobtrusive, and whenever we had visitors — after the initial greeting — she would tuck herself away in a corner content to observe. Shelties are more vociferous, giving tongue on the slightest pretext and enjoying involvement in every activity that is going on around them.

The collie standard mentions dignity and that they most certainly have, whereas the sheltie standard requires a dog 'lithe and graceful with speed and jumping power great for its size'.

The description of heads in the standards is certainly similar, but here, to my mind, is one of the major differences. The collie standard calls for a 'slight but perceptible stop' and the sheltie standard for a 'slight but definite stop'. Lack of stop is undesirable in both breeds but it is more often forgiven in the collie, possibly due to the length of head. It does not seem to detract quite so much in the collie, but lack of stop in the sheltie head, gives a hard and totally foreign look. Although the sheltie standard calls for a refined head, it is the collie head which has the length and refinement. A long refined collie head would look unbalanced and totally wrong on a sheltie.

Ears are also different. The collie standard says: 'These should be small and not too close together on top of the skull'. Whereas the sheltie standard says: 'Ears should be small, moderately wide at the base and placed fairly close together on top of the skull'.

In both cases the eye should be the same: 'Of medium size, obliquely set and of almond shape' there is nevertheless a difference in expression. The collie standard states that the expression should be: 'Full of intelligence, with a quick alert look when listening'. The sheltie standard is more elaborate: 'The expression, being one of the most marked characteristics

Sheltie head study, Aust Ch Ellendale Etienne, left Collie head study Ch Sandiacre Slap 'N' Tickle.

of the breed, is obtained by the perfect balance and combination of skull and foreface, size, shape, colour and placement of eyes, correct position and carriage of ears, all harmoniously blended to produce that almost indefinable look of sweet, alert, gentle intelligence'.

The head and expression was one of the first things that attracted me to the shetland sheepdog and I have endeavoured to maintain it in my own stock, because without it, a sheltie is just not a sheltie.

Both standards are similar regarding the requirements for body and construction with well arched necks, level backs and the body slightly longer than the height of the dog at the withers. The basic difference is that the collie should have a slight rise over the loins and the sheltie must have a graceful sweep over the loins and the croup should slope gradually to the rear.

The photographs serve to demonstrate both the differences and similarities of the two breeds, especially in the head properties. The lovely rough collie bitch Champion Sandiacre Stripper with her beautifully shaped and placed eye has a rather dignified bearing compared to the equally lovely sheltie bitch Champion Forestland Tassel who also has the desired eye shape and placement. The difference in expression is largely due to the sheltie's more definite stop and ear carriage which creates a sweet but alert look.

In comparing the outlines of the two breeds, the collie's topline has a slight rise over the loins compared to the sweep of the sheltie. In both breeds a heavy coat can often obscure the true shape and a thorough examination of the dog under the coat must be carried out to assess this. Both breeds should have a low set tail with the bone reaching at least to the hock. Nowadays we don't see many with the slight upward swirl, but there is nothing nicer than to see either breed moving soundly with a correctly carried tail. Gay tails completely spoil the symmetry of the animal.

Sable and white, tri colour and blue merle are the accepted colours in both breeds, but black and white and black and tan, although not common, are also acceptable in shelties. These latter two colours do not occur in the modern rough collie and somehow they would not look right. Having owned, bred and exhibited collies and shelties I have great affection for both and appreciate and respect the differences between them.

▼ *Diane Pearce*

*Loughrigg Blue
Rain of Ellendale
showing the correct
outline and stance.*

CHAPTER THIRTEEN

Conformation and Movement

MY idea of the perfect shape, construction and stance of the shetland sheepdog is well illustrated by the photograph of Loughrigg Blue Rain of Ellendale.

But it is vital to couple stance with showmanship. All too often you see a judge making his final assessment of a class and forgetting all about movement and construction.

He selects the dog that simply stands and shows. Many years ago a friend of mine owned a sheltie dog who had a superb front and mane and looked most impressive. But his hind action was stiff and stilted. My friend always endeavoured to be first in the line up to be examined and always showed the dog front on, and more often than not the judge had forgotten the appalling hind action by the end of the class and gave the dog first prize.

For me, showmanship is to have the dog standing right, looking alert and taking an interest in what's going on. It is not standing and gazing adoringly into the eyes of the handler. If a judge is to assess the dog's expression, it is essential that the dog looks at him. When I have been judging I have sometimes felt the only way I could assess expression would be to climb on the back of the handler. Making the dog look up always shortens the neck which is bad enough if the dog has a neck and disastrous if it hasn't. I can remember one dog who was always shown like this and apart from shortening his neck, it also showed off his complete lack of underjaw. I mentioned this, but the handler just carried on and at least three judges weren't bothered about it or the dog wouldn't have got his title.

For a dog to stand right it must be made right. It is only on rare occasions that a correctly constructed dog stands wrongly. The photograph of Loughrigg Blue Rain of Ellendale shows the correct straight front, upper arm, layback of shoulder, well bent stifle and short hock, which all contribute to a good stance and sound movement.

The gait of the shetland sheepdog should be easy and smooth, not stiff

Correct front movement.

"Paddling" — weak pasterns, out at elbows, throwing feet to the side.

Narrow front — "plaiting".

Correct rear movement.

Cowhocked.

Hocks out and toeing in.

or stilted. The correct assembly of the forehand is essential in order to obtain good positive front movement, just as the well-bent stifle and short hocks are necessary to give that smooth driving hind action. The aim is to produce the free flowing daisy cutting action, typical of the breed. The drive from the rear should be true and straight, the correct angulation and muscular development providing the means which allows the dog's hind feet to reach well under the body and push him forward.

Movement is determined by the way the dog is constructed and poor construction affects movement in various ways. For instance, slack pasterns throw the feet out almost as though they were on elastic. If the elbow joint is outward sloping it is very ugly and a dog with this fault will inevitably toe in when coming towards you. If this is combined with weak pasterns, it is even worse. Straight upper arms and shoulders produce a stilted upright action instead of the straight forward reaching action, produced with the correct upper arm and layback of shoulder. Open feet and thin weak bone also contribute to indifferent action. Hind action is seriously affected by straight stifles. These are invariably coupled with long hocks, and how ugly they look. Toeing in behind is caused by outward facing hocks, another ugly fault. Weak back ends cause cow

Correct Front.   *Out at elbows and toeing in.*   *Narrow front and weak pasterns.*

Correct rear.   *Cow hocks.*   *Legs not straight, toeing out.*

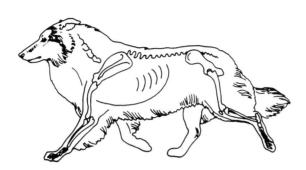

Correct movement with good forward reach and thrust from the rear.

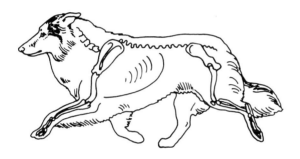

"Hackney action" — high steeping due to insufficient layback of shoulder blade and short upper arm.

"Pacing" — both legs on the same side moving in unison.

hocks. These are so often coupled with high set gay tails, another unsightly fault which completely spoils the symmetry of the outline.

If the dog has the correct fore and aft construction, good legs and feet plus the required flowing outline and a firm strong topline, it has all the ingredients for correct movement. But the remedy for improved movement, is in the hands of the breeders and judges. The breeders need to stop indiscriminate breeding and endeavour to use well bred, well constructed, sound brood bitches and stud dogs. The judges must know what is right and wrong where movement is concerned and to penalise the latter accordingly.

When I have been judging, I have been faced with some really appalling movers and I wonder whether the exhibitors of such specimens have ever taken the trouble to look at their dogs on the move. How can you know whether or not your dog is a good mover if you haven't seen him moved on a lead by another person? How often have you heard a disgruntled exhibitor coming out of the ring saying: 'He is supposed to like good movement and he's thrown me out when my dog was moving beautifully.'

This is astonishing because there is no way you can assess your dog's movement looking down on him. How can you know the correct pace for your dog if you don't watch someone else moving him? I am sure some people consider their dog has moved well as long as it moved along with them at the right pace and hasn't strayed out of line. However beautiful a sheltie may be, we have always to remember he is first and foremost a working dog.

CHAPTER FOURTEEN

Correction of Ears

DURING the teething period ears can be a real problem, up one day, down the next or one up and one down, ad infinitum. There seems to be no definite pattern where ears are concerned. Over the years I've seen prick eared dogs sire puppies with perfect ears, dogs with perfect ears sire prick eared puppies and heavy eared dogs siring puppies with neat ears. It is possible to legislate for hereditary faults like steep upper arms, shoulders and weak underjaws. But ears seem to be a law unto themselves. The one certain thing is that whenever ears go up or drop too low, they must be seen to immediately. Prompt and regular attention is absolutely vital.

In my opinion, prick ears are the easiest to deal with. I am not a believer in weighting ears as I feel this simply strengthens the ear muscles. My method is regular massage with a leather dressing such as Ko-cho-line. Apply a little to the middle of the inside of the ear then massage between finger and thumb for three or four minutes per ear, to work it right into the leather of the ear. Then fold the ear over and massage with a rolling motion. Do this at least three times a day until the ear is corrected. Some heavy coated dogs grow a tremendous amount of hair inside their ears and if this impedes the massaging, remove it. Conversely, if a puppy has neat, well placed ears and retains them through the teething period, leave well along and don't remove any hair at all until the second teeth are well and truly established.

I would not say categorically that weighting ears does not work. I have occasionally known of such things as chewing gum bring ears down. But I consider it a lazy man's way. However, if you are too busy to massage the ears and must weight them, try the same leather dressing or dubbin. Apply it to the inside of the ear and then add a small amount of fine ash to the ear tips. The leather dressing will keep the ear supple and the ash will provide a little extra weight to the ear tip. The actual amount can only be determined by trial and error.

Unfortunately ears that have been corrected by the weighting method gradually start to lift again and then you are faced with the chore of weighting the ears before every show. The massaging method is sometimes slow and laborious but once good ear carriage has been established, it seems to stay that way.

The heavy ear is a far more difficult problem to solve and luckily I have not had much experience of it. I would suggest that if a puppy's ears appear heavy before teething, it's best to wait and see as they will often lift on their own during the teething process. If this does not happen, I would suggest hard trimming of all surplus hair inside and outside the ear. Then clean the ear with a little surgical spirit to remove all natural grease and insert an oval shaped piece of chiropodist's felt or some other stiffener and secure it with sticking plaster. The top of this should reach the point at which you wish the ear to fold. Leave this in place for 48 hours. Then allow a rest period of a few days and repeat, if necessary. If sticking plaster is left on the ear indefinitely, if can cause soreness.

If you attempt this sort of treatment, you will need to isolate the puppy, otherwise you can bet your boots his kennelmates will attempt to remove whatever you have applied. The same is true if you have used grease, oil or weights. If you don't isolate the individual concerned then the other dogs will lick the grease and there is nothing more certain to cause ears to prick that constant licking. Because of this some people prefer to use a creosote based ointment, instead of grease or oil.

The small, stiff pricked ears which crops up now and again are almost hopeless from the start. These are usually thicker than the norm and because of their basic structure and placement they invariably fail to respond to treatment. Thank heavens they are few and far between. Most breeders have their own pet methods for dealing with unruly ears, many of them successful, and they are usually prepared to share their experiences with the novice.

CHAPTER FIFTEEN

Show Presentation

WHEN I first started in shelties there were few training classes and only three breed clubs. In order to learn anything about show presentation I had to rely on the very scanty literature that was available, watch experienced breeders at shows and practice hard on my own dogs. It was a case of trial and error and the more I practised the better I became. Like everything else, if you have to do it the hard way, it sticks.

The first essential is to get the dog into condition, starting with correct feeding. Good nutritious food is necessary for body, bone and coat. There is such a variety of dog food available these days and much of it very good, canned, packaged, moist, dry – and all plugged by the media in every shape and form. We still prefer to use fresh meat with tinned food as a standby. Minced ox cheek is excellent, so is paunch, otherwise known as tripe. We use all types of fish, herring in particular, vegetables, wholemeal biscuit, cereal meal and the pellet type mixer. Whatever you do, vary the diet and keep the dogs interested. Just imagine how you would feel having to eat the same thing, day in and day out. We always cook the meat or fish and the mix it with any leftover vegetables and either a mixture of biscuit and cereal mix, or mixer. We serve it just warm, particularly in the winter. We find the dogs prefer the puppy sized meal rather than the larger terrier type. We rarely feed raw meat. Quantities vary with the individual and this is often a case of trial and error. There are usually no problems when feeding a number of dogs. But with a singleton it is important not to discourage it and certainly not to overfeed. Nothing looks worse than an overweight dog.

Regular exercise and grooming are both vital ingredients for good health. Roadwork is essential for the feet and claws, although concrete or gravel runs help in this respect. It you are lucky, you will have access to woods or open farmland which you can use for free running your dogs, safely away from traffic. The dogs thoroughly enjoy this daily romp in a group. It seems to tone them up and is certainly the highlight of their day.

I always find grooming a dog is very relaxing. It was always my way of unwinding after a hard day at the office. Some dogs are a pleasure to groom and some are equally as difficult. But the earlier you start a grooming routine with a puppy, the better. Most dogs enjoy being groomed and the more often it is done, the easier it becomes. Remember, where trimming is concerned, the golden rule is little and often.

GROOMING EQUIPMENT

A good quality ladies hairbrush with natural medium bristle is the first essential. Wire brushes rip out the undercoat and can scratch the skin, and nylon brushes set up so much static in the coat that they are unworkable. Always have a couple of good metal combs with medium spaced teeth. I find bone handled combs very comfortable to use. A fine tooth comb is necessary for teasing out the soft hair at the base of the ears, which knots so easily if not combed regularly. A stripping knife, with a fine serrated edge, is the best thing for putting a nice natural finish to the hocks. You will also need a good pair of hairdressers scissors, a plastic plant spraying bottle with a fine-spraying nozzle, rain water, a liquid chalk aerosol and last but not least, a towel.

Typical example of equipment for keeping the Sheltie well groomed.

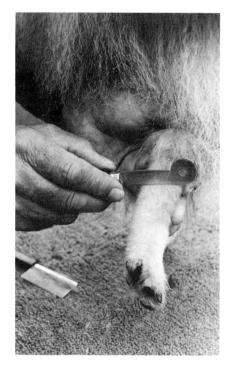

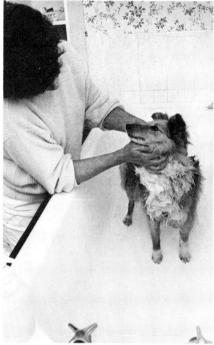

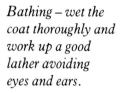

After trimming tidy up the hocks with a stripping knife.

Bathing – wet the coat thoroughly and work up a good lather avoiding eyes and ears.

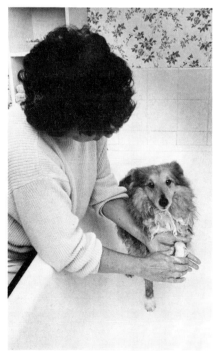

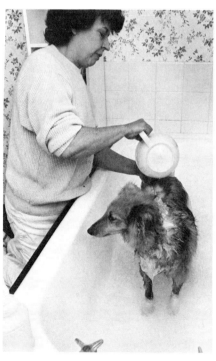

Pay special attention to legs and feet.

Use a large jug to rinse thoroughly.

Ensure the dog is completely dry before being returned to the kennel.

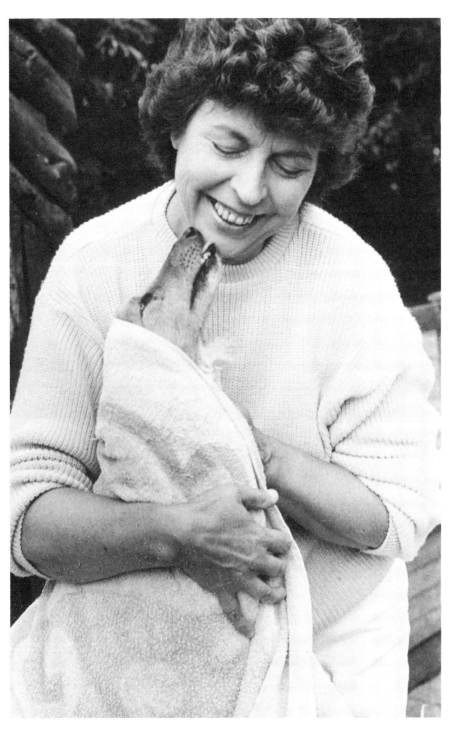

GROOMING

I prefer to do the trimming first, while the dog is completely dry. I start with the ears and using finger and thumb, with a little talcum powder to help the grip. Always trim ears outwards taking the long surplus hair and removing just a little at a time. The whole idea is to keep the ear looking as neat and natural as possible, so that when it is finished, it looks as though it has not been touched. If you find it hard going with finger and thumb, the stripping knife can be used. But you never get quite the same natural effect. Trimming ears is the most difficult job of all requiring a lot of practice and infinite patience. All ears have their differences, the size, the placement, how much they tip and how much hair they carry, and incorrect trimming can affect the outlook of the dog.

If the dog carries his ears high then only take off the very long soft surplus hair and don't remove any from the tip. If the ears are heavy then you can obviously remove more hair to improve the appearance, but don't remove so much that they look like fox terriers. I used to practice on my old dogs, non-showers and in-whelp bitches before tackling the show specimens. The golden rule is do not remove too much the first time – you cannot put it back.

After the ears the feet, and here again it is simple trimming to tidy up the foot and keep its natural oval shape. It is important to note that cat feet are not correct for the breed. Using the scissors cut away any surplus hair from the top and sides of the foot and from between the pads which can become quite profuse if not attended to frequently. Thick fur between the toes can spread the feet. Cut off any long hair growing from the heel of the front feet, if this is left it not only looks untidy, it makes the foot appear longer and if combed out, resembles a shire horse. Once the surplus hair is removed, the length of the nails must be checked and clipped back where necessary. This is quite easy with white or pink nails where the quick is apparent. But with black nails it is better to clip the point of the nail and file the rest. It is always a good idea to file all nails after clipping in order to remove sharp edges. It is absolutely essential to trim nails regularly, particularly on dogs which are kept mainly on turf or soft runs. Roadwork and concrete runs do help to keep nails down to an acceptable length.

The next job is to trim the back of the hocks. First comb the hair outwards with the fine comb, then remove the surplus hair by cutting downwards on a slightly convex curve. But do not cut too close to the bone, it is always best to leave the hair just a little longer than the ideal and then tidy it up with the stripping knife.

Teeth need regular attention. It's surprising how often they are neglected, yet cleaning them is a simple matter. I've tried salt and tooth-

Before commencing grooming spray the coat thoroughly with rain water.

After spraying lightly towel the coat.

Brush coat vigorously tail to head.

Brush the coat back in layers so that it lays the correct way making you get down to the skin.

Finish by brushing the coat to follow the body lines.

paste but the best thing I know of is a charcoal block. It is not too abrasive and the dogs soon get used to it. A large knuckle bone or a wholemeal biscuit is always appreciated and is good for keeping the teeth clean as well as relieving boredom. But these should only be left with dogs kennelled alone. Even if you supply one bone each in a group of dogs, there will always be one who thinks he should have the lot and this invariably leads to disputes. If the teeth are coated with tartar the only answer is a metal dental scaler, though some dogs object strongly to this and need to be mildly sedated. Of course, the vet will always clean and scale the teeth under anaesthetic, but prevention is better than cure, and also less expensive.

A well presented dog is in the first instance a clean dog, and here there are two schools of thought, those for bathing and those against. I am not emphatically for or against because I find, as with everything connected with shelties, you just cannot generalise. It depends on the individual dog, the type of coat, how it is kennelled, what type of run it is exercised in, and the area in which the kennel is situated. If you live in an industrial and heavily populated area then the atmospheric conditions will usually mean a grubbier coat with the necessity of more frequent bathing, whereas the

Make the most of the leg fringes, they look more profuse when tangle free.

Comb the silky hair behind the ears with a fine toothed comb.

Comb the leg fringes with a medium toothed comb.

country dog away from industrial fall-out should have a much cleaner coat and can be shown for long periods with just the occasional bath.

When it comes to bathing or any sort of cleaning the most important thing to consider is the type of coat and this varies tremendously – and I don't mean just between the colours.

You are very lucky if your dog has the correct harsh lengthy outercoat with the thick short undercoat giving the right amount of stand off. This is the coat which seems unaffected by heat or cold, dry or damp and always look healthy. Without this type of coat, you can spend hours on your dog the day before a show, and get him looking just right. Then you drive 200 miles or so, arrive at the show and out he jumps looking like a rag bag, the car heater having played havoc with the coat, and you have to start all over again.

If you decide your dog needs bathing, then regardless of the type of coat, do it at least two or three days before the show and give the coat a chance to regain its natural oils. If you do it the night before the show you will be disappointed with the result, particularly if it is hot on show day. There are many excellent brands of shampoo available with little to choose between them. But it is essential to rinse thoroughly and leave no trace on the skin. Also make sure the dog is thoroughly dried before returning to his quarters.

In view of the current ban on the use of white powder, it is always best to wash the white parts the day before the show. Much of the groundwork can also be done on pre-show day. My routine is to spray the coat completely with rain water making sure it penetrates the outer coat. Then massage and lightly towel until the coat is just damp. Brush vigorously the wrong way, that is, tail to head, and then brush lightly the opposite way, head to tail following the lines of the body. When brushing, make sure you get down through the undercoat to the skin so that the hairs are parted and the air can circulate through the coat. Rub a little talcum powder or starch into the white parts and then brush out the surplus. Comb out the leg fringes and around the ears. The skirts should be brushed upwards towards the tail, then downwards and outwards, the tail being brushed lightly towards the root then shaken out. Always use clean brushes and combs, which should be rinsed frequently in a mild antiseptic solution. On show day the aerosol whiteners are very handy. But remember the solution is liquid so give it time to dry, then brush lightly and it will bring the white up beautifully. It is interesting to note the different shades of white in individual dogs. Over the years I've seen this vary from whiter than white, to almost cream. On sables it's always seemed to me that the whitest white appears on shaded sables, nevertheless whatever shade of white it still has to be worked at if the dog is to look its best.

A little bay rum mixed with fresh water at around four parts water to one part bay rum makes a useful spray for show days and keeps the dogs smelling nice. But only use it on sables because frequent use on merles and tricolours can cause a rusty tinge.

I'm often asked about dealing with dogs in the moult, and this is where I do advocate frequent bathing, especially with bitches when they have just left a litter. As soon as I notice the undercoat loosening, I bath the dog, shampooing and rinsing twice. Then dry with a thick towel and while the coat is still damp, comb out all the loose undercoat. At this time, I use the comb far more than when the dog is in full coat. I follow the bathing and combing procedure once a week for three or four weeks, by which time all the loose coat should be cleared. The sooner this is done the quicker the new coat will come through. It is surprising that despite the moult, the hair grows just as quickly in the places where you would prefer it not to – between the pads, in and around the ears. During and immediately after the moult I add a dessertspoonful of sunflower oil to the main meal each day.

Judge Maurice Baker with International Nordic Champion Mondurles Bannock, best in show winner at the Norweigan Shetland and Sheepdog Championship Show, 1982.

Judge Maurice Baker at the 1988 Southern Counties Championship Show with Champion Daleoak Christmas Rose and Champion Mountmoor Blue Boy.

CHAPTER SIXTEEN

Judging

I HAVE been involved with shetland sheepdogs for over 30 years and I have seen many changes. Entries have increased, there are more breed clubs and there are different attitudes towards showing. But the greatest change is in the attitude towards judging.

When I started in the breed in the middle fifties, people started showing at the local 25 class sanction shows then at limited and open shows and progressed gradually to championship shows. No one expected to judge until they had shown dogs for some years. In fact, you would expect to do a five year stint, judging on the sanction, limited and open show circuit before being allowed to judge at championship level. I think that was a very good system, it was akin to serving an apprenticeship.

Nowadays I get the distinct impression that many people want to judge before they have been in the breed any length of time. That cannot be right, and it is certainly not in the interests of the breed.

It is my opinion that a specialist judge should have prepared and exhibited the breed with some significant success, before taking on a judging engagement. I think you have to put yourself in the exhibitor's position when judging in order to appreciate the problems of presentation and showmanship. You cannot do that if you have never presented or handled a dog in the ring. I also believe that the best way to develop a good eye, is to have a top class dog around the house. It is beneficial to have some stewarding experience, prior to judging. It doesn't help you to make decisions, but it does help in marshalling the ring. I also think that some club judging lists are drawn up with insufficient thought. People are allowed on to these lists, with little or no experience in the breed. That is why I have always supported the judges' training scheme, that was started by the English Shetland Sheepdog Club. It is not perfect, but it is certainly a step in the right direction.

It is important to be in the right frame of mind when judging. Remember everyone who has entered has paid the money for you to assess their dog and they all deserve the same amount of attention. Therefore, good, bad or indifferent, give them a thorough examination. You must develop a method of going over the dogs, and it must be one which suits you, so don't just copy someone else. If it is your first judging engagement, practise on your own dogs at home. Then you develop a method which soon becomes second nature. Be thorough but don't prolong it, if you have a large entry you won't have time to waste. One of my pet hates is the exhibitor who seems to think the dog should show on the table. This is completely wrong and I believe it is a total waste of time. This method of showing on the table probably developed at small shows when the exhibitor wanted to impress an inexperienced judge. Regrettably, some exhibitors and indeed some judges, seem to think it is the correct thing to do. The dog is put on the table to enable the judge to examine the construction, head profiles, teeth, ears, tail and coat – and not for showmanship.

When assessing dogs on the move, make sure each exhibitor knows exactly what you want. I prefer dogs to be moved in a triangle, then you can see everything at one go – hind action, side action and front action. I don't believe in moving the dog up and down and then sending it up again while scooting to the other side of the ring to see it in profile. You usually find that 80 per cent of exhibitors get between you and the dog. I also insist on the full use of the ring to ensure the largest possible triangle. You must also develop a good, accurate memory so you can remember how each individual moved after you've completed the class.

A final look along the line enables you to assess stance, outline, expression and the use of ears. If it is a large class of twenty to twenty-five entries, it is a good idea to shortlist about eight individuals and then request the remainder, after a word of thanks, to leave the ring. Place the selected group to one side of the ring and allow plenty of space between each dog. Then stand well back and make your final selection. Make it crystal clear who is standing first, second, third, reserve and very highly commended and when you have done that, do not start to shuffle them up and down the line. There is nothing more irritating to both exhibitors and onlookers and it smacks of indecision.

One of the most difficult decisions to make is when you run up against movement versus type. To my mind, type should come first unless the movement in a quality exhibit is really appalling. After all, a dog that looks like a donkey is capable of moving soundly. Fortunately the standard of sheltie entries is high enough so it is unlikely that you will be faced with a really black and white decision such as this and you always have the option of withholding any award, if you think this is necessary. But you will certainly be faced with the movement versus type situation, to a lesser degree. Always remember you are judging the whole dog. Evaluate the dog's good points and weigh these against the faults. But do it quickly and be decisive. The longer you look, the more difficult it becomes. Anyone can "fault-judge", but if you follow that path, you end up with a dog which is reasonably adequate in most respects but has few, if any, outstanding virtues. I remember one lovely champion dog in the north many years ago who had the most beautiful head and expression and very good conformation. But he had a slightly weak right pastern and sometimes turned his foot out. He was very often put down for this one minor fault. A genuine case of not seeing the wood for the trees.

Judges should always remember to be gentle when going over a sheltie, particularly with puppies who might be attending their first show. There is no need to be severe or grip the rib cage like a vice, you can feel the bone structure without being too firm.

I do believe it is a mistake to start judging before you have had some years experience in the show ring. Equally important, if you don't think you will enjoy judging, don't do it, you have the freedom of choice. However, once started do try and enjoy it and be pleasant. It costs nothing to smile and it means such a lot to the exhibitor, especially the beginner. Remember, the world will not come to an end if you make a mistake. We all do. Whatever you do you will be discussed and criticised, usually by the people who know the least. But if you have endeavoured to select exhibits of good type and construction, you will be applauded by the genuinely knowledgeable people. Whatever you are doing, you should try and look the part and this applies particularly to judging. You are on view to the public so you should look neat and tidy. You don't have to look as though you have stepped out of the pages of Vogue, but you are in the centre of the ring and not only your performance but your appearance will be under scrutiny.

When you are in the ring, don't think you are God Almighty, as some do. It's an honour to judge anywhere and you have a duty not only to the exhibitors, but to the club which invited you, the spectators and the dogs. Forget all you know about the previous wins of the exhibits and the exhibitors. Reputations mean nothing and if you think about them, it will only make your task more difficult. You are judging on the day and the exhibitors have entered for your opinion. They won't thank you for slavishly following others.

On the other hand, there is nothing clever about knocking a well-known winner just for the hell of it. I remember some years ago watching a judge making her debut. The best dog belonged to a prominent exhibitor but the judge placed it second behind an inferior specimen. After the judging she approached the well-known exhibitor and said: 'You had the best dog but if I'd put you first they would have said I was putting up faces.' The best dog must always go up, whether it belongs to a top exhibitor or a raw novice. After all, the seasoned exhibitor rarely goes into the ring with a third rate dog. Be calm, be pleasant, be decisive, be honest, get on with the job and don't dither and you will have the satisfaction of a job well done.

CHAPTER SEVENTEEN

Care of The Old Dog

SHELTIES are usually long lived and if cared for properly they give an awful lot in return. The first essential when the dog moves into the veteran stage is to provide warm sleeping quarters. We prefer the old dogs to have the use of the kitchen, utility room or similar. We feel they should be kept away from the hurly burly of kennels and runs, although they still come along on the walks and enjoy being part of things. As we are lucky enough to be able to walk our dogs through woods without leads, the old age pensioners can stroll along at their leisure, while the younger set gallop ahead and then come roaring back to meet us. Food is also important and with older dogs we maintain the quality but reduce the quantity slightly, we have found that little and often is generally far better than one huge meal.

When the dog's age moves into double figures there will often be dental problems and we don't hesitate to have infected teeth removed, rather than let a dog suffer pain. Abscesses under the teeth can be fairly common in an old dog and are extremely painful. Regular care and dental attention, such as scaling of teeth, is essential if infection is to be detected early and dealt with. It is surprising how quickly the gums harden after teeth have been extracted and how well the dog can cope with biscuit. However, we prefer to feed a lighter biscuit of the mixer type to the older dogs.

Regular grooming is a must, there is nothing better for making a dog feel good than a brisk walk, followed by a thorough brushing and combing. As the dog gets older, the coat seems to become more greasy and regular bathing helps to make him feel and look good. But he must be quickly dried, preferably with a hair drier in front of a good fire. When the dog is in his latter years the eyes are often gummed up in the morning. Clean this off with a wad of cotton wool, well wrung out in warm water. A smear of vaseline on the lids will stop them sticking together.

The nails also seem to grow quickly on the old dog, probably because they don't chase about enough to keep them worn down. They should be inspected and trimmed regularly for comfortable exercise. Dew claws, if not removed as a puppy, can be a problem, I've seen so many actually growing back into the leg on old dogs and what a mess they are.

This is a completely unnecessary state of affairs because it is so easy to cut them back at the same time as trimming the nails. A really good pair of nail clippers is essential as adult nails are particularly tough, the guillotine type seem to be the most successful of those we have tried.

The companionship of an old dog is something to be treasured, even if sometimes a little demanding. He will have a built-in alarm clock when it comes to feeding time, exercise time and when he gets his titbits. He will know your every move before you make it. As long as he receives the right attention, the old dog will repay you with love and affection for many years. But once he ceases to enjoy life, don't let it become a misery for him. You know when it is time to do the right thing.

CHAPTER EIGHTEEN

Best of British

IT would be impossible to illustrate all the lovely dogs I've admired during thirty years in the breed, both at home and overseas, so I have made a random selection from the dogs I have been personally involved with – those I have judged and those I have used for breeding purposes.

The incomparable Champion Helensdale Ace was the outstanding dog at the time when I was considering going into shelties, and although I never saw him, I did use him and also bought one of his daughters. Olwen Gwynne-Jones (Callart) always regarded Ace as the number one – and she should know as she has seen all the best during a lifetime in shelties. The full impact of Champion Ace on the breed has probably never been really appreciated. His influence was all the more remarkable as he was tragically poisoned when he was only six years old.

Ace was the sole product of an accidental mother to son mating. Breeder Jim Saunders told me that he had gone off one day to a local show and as it was a sunny day he had left all the dogs outside in their respective runs. Champion Helensdale Bhan was in the next run to his mother, Helensdale Gentle Lady, who happened to be in season. When Jim returned, Bhan was in the mother's run and Ace, a singleton, was the outcome of that union. This story certainly illustrates what a great part luck plays in breeding. Jim tried to register the puppy as Helensdale Lone Star but the Kennel Club would not allow this and substituted the name Ace, and what an apt choice it turned out to be. Ace sired ten champions, but what is more important, is the number of winners he is behind – it would be a virtually impossible task to calculate these. What a debt the breed owes to Jim and Ace.

Mrs J.G
Saunders
with Helensdale
Morna, the
Judge
Miss O.
Gwynne-Jones
Mr J.G. Saunders
with Ch
Helensdale Ace.

Champion HELENSDALE ACE
Born 1949

Sire: Ch Helensdale Bhan
Dam: Helensdale Gentle Lady
Breeder/Owner: James G. Saunders

Ace's feat in going best dog in show at the prestigious City of Birmingham championship show in 1951 is still regarded by many as the outstanding performance for a sheltie at an English all breed championship show. The breed judge was Miss Olwen Gwynne-Jones. Regrettably, Ace's photo's never did him justice. Just like people, some dogs are photogenic and some are not.

Champion TRUMPETER OF TOONEYTOWN (Trumpy)
Born 1959

Sire: Ch Alasdair of Tintobank
Dam: Hallinwood Sunset Gold
Breeder/Owner: Mrs Margery Guest

I loved this handsome dog from the first time I saw him, a masculine dark sable he had substance with quality and a great air of 'I'm it'. Much loved by his owner, Trumpy made his presence felt as a stud as well as a show dog and lives on in countless pedigrees both in the UK and in Australia. He became a champion within a year of making his debut at six and a half months. But like all great dogs he was a laster and he took two more challenge certificates in his later years, one being at Crufts.

Champion ELLENDALE PRIM OF PLOVERN (Prim) Born 1960

Sire: Helensdale Frolic
Dam: Kinkelbridge Foam
Breeder: Mrs J. Turner
Owner: Maurice Baker

A most glamorous sable and white with a superb temperament, Prim had a spectacular puppy career. Her many wins before she was twelve months included four reserve challenge certificates, Kennel Club junior warrant and a reserve best in show. A badly torn ligament then put her out of the ring for two years after which she came back and took two more reserve challenge certificates and three challenge certificates to gain her title, her qualifier coming at Leeds in 1965 under Sydney Meek. Unfortunately, Prim suffered from uterine inertia which severely limited her as a brood. But she did produce a few useful winners including Ellendale Crofter who won a reserve challenge certificate and Ellendale Drover who went to South Africa and took a challenge certificate.

Champion FRANCEHILL SILVERSMITH
Born 1964

Sire: Ch Dihorne Blackcap
Dam: Ch Francehill Glamorous
Breeders/owners: Mr & Mrs R. Searle

Although I had bred and exhibited blue merle rough collies, I was never really taken with blue merle shelties until I saw this dog at the Scottish Kennel Club show in 1965 where Miss Margaret Heatley awarded him his first challenge certificate. I liked both his parents and I certainly liked him. He was an ideal size, all quality, sound and eye catching. He gained his title in 1965 and the following year he was on his way to America. I always felt he would have had a marked influence on blue merle breeding if he had remained at stud in the UK.

Champion JEFSFIRE FREELANCER
Born 1966

Sire: Glenmist Golden Falcon
Dam: Ch Heathlow Luciana
Breeders/Owners: Mr & Mrs A.T. Jeffries

Freelancer was awarded five challenge certificates between 1967 and 1969 as well as taking many other awards, but it was as a stud dog that he really excelled and had a marked influence on the breed. A dominant sable and white, he stamped his type on his progeny to such a degree that he became the most successful sire in the history of the breed in the United Kingdom. He sired twelve champions — eight male and four female and three challenge certificate winners. He also sired Danish Champion Jefsfire Allanvail Gold Spark who followed in father's footsteps siring two United Kingdom champions and numerous winners in Scandinavia.

Champion ELLENDALE LISTO LUELLA (Petra)
Born 1967

Sire: Ch Greenscrees Swordsman
Dam: Gentle Adventure
Breeder: Mrs P. Stokes
Owners: Maurice Baker and Mrs M. McAdam

I purchased this charming little bitch from the breeder completely un-
shown at the age of fourteen months and she soon made her mark with best
of breed and best in show wins. I was unable to campaign her as much as I
would have liked so I let her go to Mrs M. McAdam who successfully
campaigned her to win her title. Regrettably, she had whelping problems
and was unsuccessful as a brood, she was a lovely character and ended her
days as a much loved companion.

**Champion MONKSWOOD MOSS TROOPER
Born 1967**

Sire: Ch Riverhill Raider
Dam: Ch Deloraine Dilys of Monkswood
Breeders: Mrs E.M. Knight and Miss M. Davis
Owners: Miss M. Davis

An impressive sable and white with a most lovely head and expression, this dog simply exuded quality and was always beautifully presented. I'd heard he was an indifferent showman but when I judged him at Manchester in 1970 he seemed to like me as much as I liked him. I gave him his second challenge certificate and best of breed. His most notable son was Champion Mistmere Marching Orders.

Photo Diane Pearce

Champion SCYLLA VAGUELY BLUE (Snap)
Born 1968

Sire: Strikin' Midnight at Shelert
Dam: Blue Swan at Scylla
Breeder/Owner: Mrs M.A. Marriage

This charming blue merle dog was absolutely spot on for size. Both his sire
and grandsire were prolific and successful studs, though neither were
champions. There was little to dislike about Snap apart from the fact that
he was rather too heavily marked on his left side, hence the name
"Vaguely" Blue. Following the family tradition he also was successful at
stud his progeny included the lovely blue merle bitch champion Parrocks
Possibility. Coincidentally both she and her father gained their titles on
the same day, at the Scottish Kennel Club in 1972 under Miss F.M.
Rogers.

Diane Pearce

Champion MISTMERE MARCHING ORDERS (Ross)
Born 1970

Sire: Ch Monkswood Moss Trooper
Dam: Mistmere Lysebourne Kursaal
Breeder/Owner: Mrs S.E. Harries

This handsome fellow was always superbly presented by his owner, then
Miss Sandra Tucker. The first time I saw him I was judging bitches at a
breed club show. Sitting waiting my turn, I watched this beautiful dog
come into the ring and thought: 'There is the dog challenge certificate
winner and possibly best in show'. So much for my predictions, he wasn't
even placed, perhaps for the only time in his career. I always felt he could
have been a group winner if given the chance. I never had the opportunity
of judging him until he was a veteran, but he was still capable of competing
and took a well deserved reserve challenge certificate to add to his five
challenge certificates. A somewhat reluctant stud, he nevertheless produced some quality offspring including Champion Lythwood Snaffels.

Champion MIRABELL OF MONKREDDAN
Born 1970

Sire: Peddlar of Monkreddan
Dam: Miss Muffet of Monkreddan
Breeder/owners: Mr & Mrs J. Caldwell

This particular bitch was a great favourite of mine and is featured as a tribute to the late Madge and Jack Caldwell. We were friends for many years and seemed to see the breed through the same eyes.

Madge and Jack established the most successful sheltie kennel in Scotland after the Helensdales, their dogs were all of a type, mostly golden sables, always beautifully presented and handled by Madge.

The Monkreddan dogs live on in many pedigrees around the world and their owners in many memories.

**Champion FELTHORN BEACHCOMBER (Everard)
Born 1972**

Sire: Troubleshooter of Shemaur
Dam: Felthorn April Dancer
Breeders/Owners: Mr & Mrs R. Thornley

I did not really get to know this dog until his show days were over, but
when I did, I was so impressed with his soundness, superb construction
and temperament. He became a friend and occasionally slept in my bed-
room. He seemed to please specialists and all-rounders alike, taking seven
challenge certificates including best in show at the English Shetland
Sheepdog Club championship show and best of breed at Crufts. A most
able stud dog and sire of Champion Francehill Beach Boy, among others.

LINVALLEA GOLD SPICE
Born 1972

Sire: Westaglow Khalif
Dam: Westaglow Joyful
Breeder/Owner: Mrs L. Blackgrove

If ever a bitch deserved to be a champion, it was this lovely sable and
white. She has been a model of consistency in the show ring from the age of
six months when she commenced her career with a best puppy win, up to
the present day when at nearly sixteen years she is still taking the top spot
in veteran classes. I coveted her the first time I judged her in 1975 at
National Working Breeds show and have twice made her best veteran in
show. She has a reserve challenge certificate to her credit and her owner
tells me she is a perfect companion.

**Champion SHELDERON GAY GHILLIE
Born 1973**

Sire: Ch Jefsfire Freelancer
Dam: Shelderon Corrie Crioch
Breeder/owner: Mrs Sheila McIntosh

This Freelancer son was a great favourite of mine. I judged him twice giving him best of breed at an open show and later the challenge certificate at seven years of age at Belfast championship show in 1980. He was an outgoing dog who loved obedience work as well as shows and passed his happy disposition on to his children. It was a great pity when a necessary operation cut short his stud career but it extended his life span and he is still going strong at fifteen and a half years old.

Graham Russell

Champion MIDNITESUN JUSTIN TIME
Born 1973

Sire: Midnitesun Good News
Dam: Midnitesun Party Piece
Breeder/Owner: Mrs R. Wilbraham

A masculine shaded sable grandson of Champion Trumpeter of Tooney-town and not unlike him. Not a glamour boy, but hard to fault with a quality head, beautiful construction, great coat, movement and presence. He was not campaigned non-stop, but nevertheless accumulated eleven challenge certificates. I had the pleasure of awarding him his sixth challenge certificate and best of breed at the National Working Breeds championship show in 1975. If my arm was twisted, I might say he was the best overall sheltie I have ever judged. He was a great stud, siring champions at home and abroad.

Champion MARKSMAN OF ELLENDALE (Ben)
Born 1974

Sire: Ch Scarabrae Statesman
Dam: Plovern Pearl
Breeder: Mrs L. Coverdale
Owners: Mr and Mrs M. Baker

The breeder of this dog does not know he is a champion. She only bred one litter as she wanted another bitch. I bred his grandmother, so Mrs Coverdale therefore came to me for advice on a stud dog and I recommended Statesman. The dam was five years old when mated and had one bitch and three dogs. I first saw the litter at seven weeks and Ben absolutely stood away. A dog with a faultless head and eye, lovely size, coat and a very free mover. He is the only sheltie to have won best in show at three consecutive breed club open shows. A dog with a most lovable temperament, he is still winning at fourteen years of age. He excelled as a stud with numerous winners including four UK and two overseas champions and many reserve challenge certificate winners.

Champion FRANCEHILL BEACH BOY (Boy)
Born 1974

Sire: Ch Felthorn Beachcomber
Dam: Francehill Edelweis
Breeder/Owner: Mrs M. Searle

The glamour boy of the Francehill kennel and typical of the type and
quality one associates with this prefix. I fell for him at first sight and gave
him the reserve challenge certificate at National Working Breeds in 1975
and it took the great Justin Time to beat him. Altogether he took seven
challenge certificates and five reserve challenge certificates and was the
sire of three British champions. Boy was a delightful character with a great
affinity to children, a point which worried his owner as he would stop
showing and want to play if any kids appeared at the ringside. A happy and
much loved family dog.

Champion JASMINE OF JANETSTOWN
Born 1975

Sire: Lysebourne Quick March
Dam: Janetstown Japonica
Breeder: Mrs L. Frosch
Owner: Mrs J. Moody

I had the opportunity of watching this bitch develop from a lovely puppy into the outstanding specimen she became. I made her best puppy and best of breed at Buckinghamshire Canine Society in 1976 and predicted a bright future for her. Seven years later in 1983 she came under me at the West of England Ladies Kennel Society show in what the breed statistician assured me was a world record entry for the breed under a single judge, and took a well deserved best of breed. By then she had developed into the mature, hard to fault showgirl with all the virtues. Her owner told me she was a show-off, being quiet at home, but rising to the occasion and coming alive in the show ring. It is interesting to note how closely the paternal side of her pedigree resembles that of Champion Shetlo Sheraleigh. Jasmine accumulated ten challenge certificates, a record for a sable and white bitch.

B.D.M. Photograph

ELLENDALE BOATMAN (Regal)
Born 1975

Sire: Ch Scarabrae Statesman
Dam: Ellendale Entanglement
Owner: Miss K. Vooght
Breeder: Maurice Baker

This attractive heavily coated sable dog, half brother to Champion Marks-
sman of Ellendale, was sold to his owner as an eight week old puppy and
became her friend and favourite companion until he died in 1988 Due to
his owner's domestic commitments he was never fully campaigned, but
he nevertheless gained three reserve challenge certificates and over sixty
best of breed wins at open shows. Regal was a mischievous character
with a great zest for life.

Champion SHETLO SHERALEIGH (Fleur)
Born 1975

Sire: Moonraker from Mistmere
Dam: Exbury Larkspur
Breeder/Owner: Mrs D.H. Moore

A most feminine and delightful sable and white, a truly ideal showgirl because she was so full of personality. She was the correct size with a most lovely head and expression and always beautifully presented. She took seven challenge certificates and I had the pleasure of judging her at the English Shetland Sheepdog Club championship show in 1978 where she was on top form. In conjunction with Miss Ferelith Hamilton, I made her best in show. She was successful as a brood, producing Champion Shetlo The Gay Piper.

Champion MYRIEHEWE FANTASIA
Born 1975

Sire: Ch Ferdinando of Myriehewe
Dam: Drannoc Flower Girl
Breeder/Owner: Miss I. Beaden

This lovely sable and white bitch was a great favourite of mine, like the great Helensdale Ace she was produced from a mother and son mating and absolutely exuded quality. I gave her a challenge certificate at Paignton in 1979 and then much later I gave her best of breed when she was a veteran at Anglesey in 1982.

Champion SNABSWOOD SLAINTHE (Glen)
Born 1976

Sire: Ch Greenscrees Nobleman
Dam: Snabswood Sally Anne
Breeder/Owner: Mr R.G. Fitzsimons

A lovely sable and white dog with an air of quality, he had a most successful puppy career and gained his title in 1977. He was given his third
challenge certificate at the Shetland Sheepdog Club of Wales under the
late Mrs M. Henry. I was judging bitches and agreed to make him best in
show. The following year I had the pleasure of awarding him his fourth
challenge certificate at the English Shetland Sheepdog Club in a lovely
entry. Sire of the elegant Champion Snabswood Summer Wine.

Champion LYTHWOOD SNAFFELS
Born 1976

Sire: Ch Mistmere Marching Orders
Dam: Drannoc Silhouette of Lythwood
Breeder/Owner: Mr D. Rigby

A beautifully marked sable and white of great charm and elegance, beautifully coated with a lovely head and expression. I gave him best dog at the
Yorkshire Shetland Sheepdog Club open show and then he took four
challenge certificates in 1979. His early death was a great loss to the breed.
The Lythwood kennel is renowned for its type and quality and is the only
kennel to have bred four male champions in direct line, a most outstanding breeding achievement.

W.G. Russell

Champion HAYTIMER OF HANBURYHILL AT HARTMERE (Ricky)
Born 1977

Sire: Ch Riverhill Ricotta
Dam: Hanburyhill Honeysuckle
Breeder: Mrs R. Archer
Owners: Mr & Mrs Hart and Rev & Mrs Hanbury

A richly coloured sable and white, full of type and ring presence and absolutely spot on for size. Apart from his successful show career, he made his mark as a stud. He was the sire of four UK champions, three Norwegian champions plus numerous challenge certificate and reserve challenge certificate winners. His early retirement from stud was a great blow to the breed but he lives life to the full, a much loved family favourite and a great character.

Champion SHEMAUR NOEL EDMONDS (Noel)
Born 1977

Sire: Ch Midnitesun Justin Time
Dam: Shemaur Midnight Melody
Breeder: Mrs S.A. Baker
Owners: Mr & Mrs M. Baker

The only champion son of Justin Time in the UK, a tri colour who was never out of coat, a superb mover of correct size but with plenty of substance. He was not the best of showmen but was sheltie of the year in 1978 and finally after a long campaign took his three challenge certificates in 1982. A most efficient stud and father of champions at home and abroad.

Champion JOYWIL JEANETA
Born 1978

Sire: Jefsfire Sweepstake of Joywil
Dam: Joywil Jasmin
Breeder/owner: Mrs J. Seaman.

I first saw this most attractive little bitch at the English Shetland Sheepdog
Club championship show in 1978 where Miss Frerelith Hamilton and I
made her best minor puppy in show. She was handled that day by Eric
Seaman.
She was a personality plus girl and arguably the best to come from the
Joywil kennel. She soon gained her title and went on to become a success-
ful brood bitch.

Champion PHILHOPE STARDUST
Born 1977

Sire: Rodhill Clouded Apollo
Dam: Philhope Rollin' Star
Breeder: Mrs P.Q. Pierce
Owners: Mr & Mrs M. Hart

I am pleased to feature this beautiful sable and white as a tribute to one of the nicest people in the breed, namely the late and much loved Phyl Pierce. A staunch supporter of the breed, always helpful and approachable and invariably good humoured. Phyl sold Stardust as a puppy to her close friends Malcolm and Patti Hart and she could not have been in better hands. Always immaculately presented, she reached her peak in 1980 when she took the challenge certificate. She was still in superb condition at nine years old when my wife Sheila made her best veteran at the Mid Western Shetland Sheepdog Club championship show in 1985 and described her as the Joan Collins of the sheltie world.

Champion HERRIOT OF HERDS
Born 1981

Sire: Riverhill Ringer
Dam: Hesitation of Herds
Breeder/owner: Miss M. Gatheral

I judged this impressive tri colour dog at a Northern Counties Shetland Sheepdog Club open show and made him best dog and best opposite sex. He has great ring presence and his workmanlike appearance appealed particularly to all-rounders resulting in a number of best in show wins as well as his eight challenge certificates. A very efficient and successful sire.

Champion PEPPERHILL BLUE FIZZ
Born 1981

Sire: Solata Jet Set
Dam: Royal Sheena of Hilmisk
Breeders: Mr and Mrs Daniels
Owner: Mrs L.Sorockyj

Without doubt the best blue merle dog I've judged, what more does one say about the breed's current record holder with twenty one challenge certificates? A dog with a big ring temperament and a great ambassador for the breed. He had the lot and is a great credit to his breeders and owner. To date, he has produced two champion blue merle bitches.

Champion SILVER LADY OF STORNAWAY
Born 1981

Sire: Shelridge Gatecrasher
Dam: Felthorn Princess Ida
Breeder: Miss D.F. Bentley
Owner: Mrs Betty Gibbens

I first saw this glamorous blue merle at Dartford Open Show in 1984 where my wife Sheila made her best of breed and I gave her reserve best in show. Later at Darlington I had the pleasure of awarding her first challenge certificate and best of breed and she was later short-listed in the group. She took best of breed with all her three challenging certificates and was best in show at Chertsey Open Show in 1985. She is a lovely colour and a superb mover. Apart from her many awards in the show ring she is also the dam of Champion Stornaway Star Spangled.

Champion DUNBECK DANCING MASTER
Born 1981

Sire: Coalacre Casanova
Dam: Alwillans Melvas Wine
Breeder/Owner: Mr W.H. Hickson

A sable and white dog without any exaggeration, beautifully balanced with extra good upper arm and shoulder, sweet head, good harsh coat, never overlong but always adequate. I gave him a challenge certificate in 1985 at Darlington and the following year had the pleasure of agreeing to him being best in show at the North Wales Shetland Sheepdog Club championship show.

Diane Pearce

Champion FELTHORN BUTTON MOON (Buttons)
Born 1982

Sire: Shelbrook Moonlighting
Dam: Felthorn Marionette
Breeders/Owners: Mr and Mrs R. Thornley

Blue merle with a most engaging personality, pretty and feminine with a sweet expression and entirely sound. I gave her a reserve challenge certificate as a junior at Blackpool early in 1984 and she quickly went on to gain her title in the same year. A great character and proving to be an excellent brood. A full sister to Australian Champion Felthorn Harvest Moon and one of four champions bred the same way, quite an achievement.

G.T. Roberts

**Champion DALEOAK CHRISTMAS ROSE (Amber)
Born 1982**

Sire: Ch Marksman of Ellendale
Dam: Daleoak Damask Rosemary
Breeders/Owners: Mr & Mrs L. Walton

A classic example of line breeding, Amber has been a consistent winner since I gave her first in a minor puppy class of twenty-one on her debut. Her dam Rosemary, also a championship show winner, is a daughter of Champion Scarabrae Sinjon, a lovely headed dog. When awarding Amber her second challenge certificate, judge Derek Smith highlighted her beautifully moulded head, correct eye shape and placement, giving a gorgeous expression. I could only endorse his opinion when awarding her qualifying challenge certificate to give her dedicated owners their first champion after many years of exhibiting. Amber's full sister Daleoak Damask Rosita is also a reserve challenge certificate winner.

Diane Pearce

Champion SOLVEIG OF SNABSWOOD
Born 1982

Sire: Ch Marksman of Ellendale
Dam: Ch Snabswood Summer Wine at Willow Tarn
Breeder: Mrs R. Crossley
Owner: Mr R. Fitzsimons

A glamorous sable and white with a most attractive outline and superb head, eye and expression. A free mover, particularly good behind, doubly champion-bred and looked it. After a successful puppy career she took her title very quickly with four challenge certificates in 1984. She has already started to make her mark as a brood.

Diane Pearce

**Champion ROCKAROUND NIGHTHAWK
Born 1983**

Sire: Forestland Poacher
Dam: Rockaround Bluetta
Breeder/Owner: Mrs J. Angell

One of the best tri colour dogs in my time in the breed, his sweeping
outline and superb movement is exactly what the standard requires. A
most elegant dog with a lovely jet black coat, always beautifully presented.
Gained his title in 1986 and went on to take six challenge
certificates. A most efficient stud who stamps his type on his progeny.

Ernest T. Gasgoigne

Champion SULASGEIR TALAMBA OF SHEMAUR (Daniel)
Born 1983

Sire: Ch Marksman of Ellendale
Dam: Sulasgeir Topaz
Breeder: Mrs C. Firman
Owners: Mr and Mrs M. Baker

Without doubt the fittest and most ebullient dog I've ever had the pleasure of owning, with an extrovert temperament and a real love of life. His overall sheltie type appealed to specialists and all rounders alike. Suffice to say, he took eleven challenge certificates, nine reserve certificates and five best in shows. His outstanding achievement was being awarded the dog challenge certificate at the English Shetland Sheepdog Club championship show in 1986 by Miss Olwen Gwynne-Jones and then going best in show. Like Blue Fizz, he was late starting his stud career but his youngsters are now making their mark.

Photo David J. Lindsay

Champion SHELDERON KIRI
Born 1983

Sire: Ch Salroyds Buzzer
Dam: Dunsinane Misty Memories
Breeder/owner: Mrs Sheila McIntosh

My wife and I have a personal interest in Kiri as we sold her dam to Sheila as a nine month old puppy. Kiri is a charming little character with an engaging personality which endears her to everyone. Her show career has been consistently good so much so that she has accumulated eleven challenge certificates and six reserve challenge certificates, a record in the breed for a bitch. Sheila says she adores puppies, so I am sure we shall see some of her children following her footsteps.

Champion WILLOW TARN TEAR MARIA
Born 1983

Sire: Ch Forestland Target
Dam: Ch Snabswood Summer Wine at Willow Tarn
Breeder/Owner: Mrs R. Crossley

Charming sable and white, gorgeous type and ideal size, she stole my heart
and I made her best sheltie puppy at Blackpool in 1984. An outstanding
puppy, her show career was regrettably interrupted due to her owner's
illness. As a result she was not as extensively campaigned as she might
have been but nevertheless gained her title in 1986 getting her qualifying
challenge certificate under Miss Olwen Gwynne-Jones. One of many
outstanding shelties to bear this prefix.

Champion SHELRIDGE CEILIDH
Born 1984

Sire: Ch Shetlo The Gay Piper
Dam: Shelridge Soothsayer
Breeder/owner: Mrs C. Aaron

This beautiful sable and white was no great lover of the show ring other-wise she would have gained her title before she did. On the days when she condescended to show off her charms she looked an absolute picture and deservedly became her owner's first champion after many years of cam-paigning quality shelties. Ceilidh looks the sort to breed on.

Photo David Dalton

Champion MOUNTMOOR BLUE BOY (Bobby)
Born 1986

Sire: Ch Longdells Petrocelli
Dam: Shelridge Carte Blanche at Mountmoor
Breeder/Owner: Mrs C. A. Ferguson

This handsome blue merle was a slow developer but I liked him from the first time I saw him and was pleased when I was able to give him his qualifying challenge certificate and best of breed at Southern Counties where later he was runner up in the group. A beautifully balanced dog, who with a little more ring presence, would be in the Blue Fizz class.

D.K. MacMillan

BECKWITH BIT OF GLAMA GIRL
Born 1987

Sire: Finnish Ch Bit of A Mischief at Beckwith
Dam: Herds Heatherbelle at Beckwith
Breeders/owners: Mr & Mrs D.K. MacMillan

I felt that at least one puppy had to be featured in this section and for this I chose the lovely sable and white Beckwith Bit Of A Glama Girl. I made her best puppy at Southern Counties Championship show 1988 after she headed what was probably the best bitch puppy class I had seen in over twenty-eight years of judging the breed. She has been best puppy on many occasions and qualified for her junior warrant at nine months. Glama Girl is so full of quality and charm and is one of a continuous string of winners produced by her dedicated breeders who are great students of pedigrees.

CHAPTER NINETEEN

Shelties in Scandinavia

I HAVE been most fortunate to be involved with shelties in Scandinavia for many years. I first judged in Norway in 1972 and have been there every year since then. I am proud indeed of the close and valued friendships that have been built up over the years through a common interest in our lovely breed.

Apart from the dogs, my work in the shipbuilding industry has taken me to all the Scandinavian countries, the first visit was to Finland in 1970. So much of the Scandinavian way of life appeals to me, the friendliness of the people, the cleanliness, the fjords, the mountains, the music, the ships, the housing, the food, the uncluttered roads, none of the overcrowding we have here in the United Kingdom. I would be hard put to nominate my favourite Scandinanvian city, Helsinki, Gothenburg and Copenhagen in particular, all have their appeal. But Oslo, because of the frequency of my visits and the friends I have there, has become almost a second home to me.

Having judged regularly for so many years I have watched with great interest the progress and improvement in the breed, particularly in Norway where they have used their imported dogs so well. The same applies to Sweden and the illustrations will bear out the quality they now possess, good enough to compete anywhere.

This standard hasn't been achieved by chance but by judicious use of the best stud dogs of which there is a much smaller but perhaps more select pool than we have in the United Kingdom, where if anything we are spoiled for choice. There is also less indiscriminate breeding than occurs in the UK. In Norway for instance, their judging systems requires the judge to not only place the winners in each class but also grade each and every exhibit to laid down quality levels — one, two and three — and also to write a detailed critique on each dog. Dogs and bitches must be shown and graded at least to second quality before any of their progeny can be registered with the Norweigan Kennel Club which certainly help to maintain a minimum level.

English, Nordic, International and Finnish Champion
ELLINGTON ENDLESS FOLLY (Tracey) (Norway)
Born 1965

Sire: Ellington Elliston
Dam: Skippool Queen
Breeder: Mr J. Cartmel
Owner in UK: Mrs E. Fishpool
Owner in Norway: Miss Kari Schulstad

Tracey won numerous best of breeds up to the age of eight years and was many times placed in groups at international championship shows. She was the first sheltie in Norway to go best in show at a national championship show. I had the pleasure of grooming her prior to one of her best of breed and group wins. She was a sweet natured bitch with lots of personality and helped to put shelties on the map in Norway.

Wilhelm Dufwa

**International Nordic Champion ELLINGTON EARLY RISER
(Norway)
Born 1967**

Sire: Ellington Express
Dam: Golden Vanity
Breeder: Mrs F. Bradley
Owner in UK: Mrs E. Fishpool
Owner in Norway: Miss Kari Schulstad

Early Riser won her international title in 1971. She and her kennelmate
Ellington Endless Folly were the only female shelties to hold this title until
1976. She was a sweet feminine sheltie of lovely type and the dam of a
Norwegian/Swedish champion.

Nordic Champion MIDNITESUN TALK OF THE TOWN
(Norway)
Born 1971

Sire: Midnitesun Good News
Dam: Kyleburn Mignonette
Breeder: Mrs R. WIlbraham
Owner: Miss Kari Schulstad

Purchased from the Midnitesun kennels, Talk of the Town soon made his presence felt in Norway. I gave him best of breed and placed him in the group in Ekeberg at the Norwegian Kennel Club international championship show in 1975. He was often placed in groups and became a successful stud siring seven Norwegian champions, one Swedish/Norwegian champion and numerous challenge certificate winning children.

Norwegian Champion LYTHWOOD HAMISH
Born 1972

Sire: Ch Lythwood Brandy Snap
Dam: Lythwood Samantha Star
Breeder: Mr D. Rigby
Owner: Ove Hjelleset

I first saw this dog as a puppy at Manchester championship show and purchased him for my good friend Ove Hjelleset. He won three challenge certificates in Norway the same year. Over the next two years he collected another six challenge certificates, three of these coming from British judges. A dog with a happy temperament and a much loved family pet.

**Norwegian Champion PLOVERN PERSUASIVE (Penny)
Born 1972**

Sire: Crosstalk Gamekeeper
Dam: Plovern Petronella
Breeder: Mrs J. Turner
Owner: Kari Schulstad

This pretty little bitch was first shown at six months at Whitby Open
Show, Yorkshire, on August 9, 1972 and was placed first in the puppy
class. The judge was Kari Schulstad who later that day purchased her
and took her back to Norway and within two years she gained her title.
Penny was a great grand-daughter of Champion Ellendale Traveller and
much like him in type and temperament.

International and Nordic Champion SHELFRECT STROLLER (Sweden)
Born 1975

Sire: Ch Midnitesun Justin Time
Dam: Ch Shelfrect Sunlit Suzanne
Breeders: Mr and Mrs P.N. Fletcher
Owner: Gunilla Thiger

This doubly champion-bred sable and white dog, is one of Scandinavia's leading sires with sixteen champion children to his name, and coming from such illustrious parentage it is hardly surprising. One of only two champion males to be sired by Champion Justin Time (the other being Champion Shemaur Noel Edmonds) he stamped his type on most of his litters. His influence on the breed throughout Scandinavia has been tremendous and their gain has certainly been our loss.

**International Nordic Champion DELORAINE DOG STAR
(Gangster) (Sweden)
Born 1975**

Sire: Felthorn Indian Ink
Dam: Sukisu Dawn Melody
Breeder: Mrs F. Chapman
Owners: Monica Holmquist and Anna Uthorn

This impressive and aptly named tri colour dog was exported to Sweden
by Flo Chapman. The photograph illustrates only too well Dog Star's
excellent construction. He was a superb mover and made his mark in the
show ring throughout Scandinavia. He was also a most prolific and
successful stud, siring twelve champions as well as other winners.

**Norwegian champion LUCKY HILLS GOLDEN QUEEN
(Norway)
Born 1976**

Sire: Nordic Ch Midnitesun Talk Of The Town
Dam: Eliza of Ellendale
Breeders: Norma and Svein Rognøy
Owner: Ann-Marie Johnsen

Golden Queen is another top quality sable and white bitch of ideal size and
lovely type. I gave her the challenge certificate and best of breed at the
Norwegian Kennel Club championship show in Moss in 1977 and she was
also best in show at the Norwegian Shetland Sheepdog Club championship show in 1979 when the judge was the late and much respected Phyl
Pierce (Philhope). A repeat mating also produced a champion in Lucky
Hills Klondike. This was personally very gratifying, as I sold the dam to
the breeders and had given the sire a challenge certificate.

**International and Nordic Champion RHINOG THE
GUARDIAN (Sweden)
Born 1976**

Sire: Ch Rhinog The Black Watch
Dam: Such a Myth at Shelert
Breeder: Miss D.A. Blount
Owners: Birgitta and Per Svarstad

The photograph of this handsome tri-colour was taken when he was twelve
years old proving what a great laster he is. A multiple challenge certificate
winner, sire of numerous champions and a great character. He has had a
considerable influence on the breed and belying his age, continues to hold
his own in the show ring even today.

**Nordic Champion MOONLIGHT MADONNA (Donna) (Sweden)
Born 1978**

Sire: Int Nordic Ch Allanvail Gold Express
Dam: Dippersmoor Debutant of Jefsfire
Breeder: Eva Lundberg
Owner: Madelaine Lund

I first came across this beautiful sable and white bitch in Lilliehamar in
1981 when I was judging at the Norwegian Kennel Club championship
show. I gave her the challenge certificate and best of breed. Later, she was
placed in the group and I had the opportunity of making the acquaintance
of her charming owner Madelaine Lund who is now a much respected
friend. Madonna is as good a bitch as I've ever judged, excelling in breed
type and quality. She would be a champion in any company.

International Nordic Champion INGLESIDE COPPER IMAGE (Copper) (Sweden)
Born 1978

Sire: Shelfrect Mr Softee
Dam: Golden Galaxy of Ingleside
Breeder: Mrs S. Harries
Owners: Birgitta and Per Svarstad

This beautifully bred grandson of Champion Midnitesun Justin Time certainly made an impact on his arrival in Sweden. An upstanding dog with a lovely head and a most attractive outline, he stamped himself on his progeny both in Sweden and Norway, siring six international champions, many champions and numerous other winners.

**Norwegian Champion SHEMAUR SUCH A NIGHT (Gavin)
(Norway)
Born 1979**

Sire: Ch Shemaur Noel Edmonds
Dam: Shemaur So Lyrical
Breeder: Mrs S.A. Baker
Owners: Berit and Bjorn Johansen

An attractive rich shaded sable and white who finished up both in colour
and type very much like his grandsire Champion Midnitesun Justin Time.
A dog of correct size excelling in body, bone and coat texture. A prolific
sire of winners including the first wheaten champion in Norway – Champion Sheltiestars Such A Charmer. When he won the progeny class at the
Norwegian Sheltie Club championship show it was fascinating to see the
variety of colours in his progeny ranging from wheaten through to golden,
shaded sable and tri colour.

Norwegian Champion SHEMAUR ANGEL EYES (Liza)
(Norway)
Born 1979

Sire: Felthorn Diplomat
Dam: Shemaur Roxy Music
Breeder: Mrs S.A. Baker
Owners: Ingrid and Frode Myklebostad

A quality bitch of ideal size with a lovely temperament, a real laster, gaining her title at eight years old. She proved her worth as a brood by producing Champion Tooniehill Active Fighter and Champion Tooniehill Bright Guardian.

**International Nordic Champion MONDURLES BANNOCK
(Roscoe) (Norway)
Born 1979**

Sire: Ch Francehill Andy Pandy
Dam: Stationhill Yolanda
Breeder: Mrs M. Duralski
Owners: Aud Jorun and Helge Lie

Arguably the best British male sheltie to be exported to Norway, I gave
him his first challenge certificate at the Norwegian Kennel Club championship show at Lillehamar in 1981. He then went on to become a best in
show, group winner and multiple CACIB (international challenge certificate) winner to break every record for the breed in Norway. A very
difficult dog to fault. He was a natural showman with great ring presence,
and was always handled and presented to perfection by Aud Jorun Lie.
His fabulous show career is only equalled by his prowess at stud. He is the
sire of seventeen champions and numerous challenge certificate winners
to date.

Paul Scott

Norwegian Champion SHELTIESTARS SUCH A CHARMER (Norway)
Born 1980

Sire: Nor Ch Shemaur Such a Night
Dam: Nor Ch Lythwood Summertime
Breeders: Berit and Bjorn Johansen
Owner: Karin Martinsen

The first and only wheaten champion to date, in Norway. This doubly champion-bred dog has so much quality, particularly in head, eye and expression, with the superb pigmentation possessed by all wheatens. He won his qualifying challenge certificate at the Norwegian Shetland Sheepdog Club championship show in 1982 when Margaret Dobson was judging. Unfortunately, perhaps because his colour is rarely seen in Scandinavia, he has never had the opportunity to prove himself at stud. A great pity, as with his breeding, he would have done well.

Norwegian Champion SHMOON SPORTSMAN (Norway)
Born 1980

Sire: Ch Marksman of Ellendale
Dam: Snabswood Suchard
Breeder: Mrs M. Mooney
Owners: H. Refsland and K. Korneliussen

I coveted this sable and white dog when I first judged him as a seven months puppy and was disappointed when he was exported to Norway. However, he quickly made his presence felt there picking up three challenge certificates and two CACIBs. Unfortunately he is kennelled in a rather remote area which limits his stud work.

Norwegian Champion CANYON HOLLY HOBBY (Norway) Born 1981

Sire: Int Nordic Ch Ingleside Copper Image
Dam: Nor Ch Canyon Bonny Lass
Breeders: Inger and Jan Nyberg
Owner: Inger Hagen

A beautifully bred bitch and a most consistent winner over the years. My wife Sheila gave her reserve best of breed at the Norwegian Shetland Sheepdog Club championship show in 1984 and I placed her first in the champions class at the Norwegian Kennel Club championship show in Oslo in 1986 when she was five years old. Probably the best of a long string of winners produced by the Canyon Kennel.

International Nordic Champion THOCO'S LITTLE IMAGE LOVER (Norway)
Born 1982

Sire: Int Nord Ch Ingleside Copper Image
Dam: Nord Ch Thoco's Indian Image
Breeder and owner: Brit Unni Bolgnes

A lovely feminine sable and white great granddaughter of Champion Midnitesun Justin Time. I loved her and gave her the challenge certificate and best of breed in Bergen in 1982. She won four challenge certificates and five CACIBs and she was the first Norweigan bred bitch to become an International Nordic Champion. She is also the dam of three champions and two challenge certificate winners.

Norwegian Champion TITT-FRAM'S HAPPY DAY (Norway) Born 1982

Sire: Int Nord Ch Shelgate Double Diamond
Dam: Tim-Tim's Tarina
Breeders: Tove & Terje Skjønhaug
Owners: Ragnhild Lunde & Tove Skjønhaug

A most elegant bitch and one of the most successful blue merles in Norway. Doubly line bred to International Nordic champion Deloraine Dog Star and obviously inheriting his show personality. I judged her in 1986 and admired her type and presence.

Norwegian Champion TOONIEHILL ACTIVE FIGHTER (Solon) (Norway)
Born 1983

Sire: Nor Ch Shemaur Such A Night
Dam: Nor Ch Shemaur Angel Eyes
Breeders: Ingrid and Frode Myklebostad
Owners: Anne and Odd Nygaardsmoen

An elegant golden sable and white with a really good neck and lovely head and eye, he completed his title in 1985. A good example of line breeding, he looks capable of producing quality if given the right bitches.

THOCO'S VICTORIAN STYLE (Sweden)
Born 1986

Sire: Int and Nordic Ch Shelfrect Stroller
Dam: Int and Nordic Ch Thoco's Little Image Lover
Breeders: Brit-Unni and Rolf Bolgnes
Owner: Gunilla Thiger

This lovely young doubly champion-bred sable and white bitch is a typical example of the quality now being produced in Scandinavia. Apart from her physical attributes, she has a gorgeous temperament. It is interesting that her three challenge certificates to date have all been awarded by British judges – namely Albert Wight, Malcolm Hart and Sheila Ann Baker.

CHAPTER TWENTY

Best of the rest

**International Champion HONEYBOY OF CALLART (Simon)
Born 1962**

Sire: Ch Miel of Callart
Dam: Tamera of Callart
Breeder/Owner in UK: Miss Olwen Gwynne-Jones
Owners in Canada: Mrs G. Fountain and Miss Gill Shields

I first saw Honeyboy as a puppy at a breed show where I was stewarding and immediately marked him down as a dog to use. But alas, before the opportunity arose, he had departed for Canada. Our loss was Canada's gain, he soon became a champion there and went on to sire eleven champions and numerous other winners. A high quality dog with a huge coat of bright red gold, he was the third champion tail male to be bred by Olwen Gwynne-Jones.

**English and Australian Champion RIVERHILL RAMPION (Tam)
Born 1966**

Sire: Stalisfield Samphire
Dam: Ch Riverhill Rather Nice
Breeders/Owners in UK: The Misses P.M. & F.M. Rogers
Owners in Australia: Helen and Edward Clinton

I had the pleasure of giving this beautifully bred dog his qualifying challenge certificate at Blackpool in 1968. Shortly afterwards he left for Australia and as his new owners said, he proved to be the right dog in the right place at the right time.

Having Champion Trumpeter of Tooneytown as his grandsire and the very best of the Riverhills on his maternal side, he combined so well with earlier imports and their progeny to the extent that he sired thirty-six champions — twenty male and sixteen female. He was Stud Dog of the Year in 1971, 1972 and 1973, runner-up in 1974-5 and outright winner in 1976. In a recent survey of Australian and New Zealand champions pedigrees, Rampion was found to be in some four hundred of these. A truly remarkable record and one is left to ponder on just what influence he might have had, had he remained in the United Kingdom. Tam lived a happy and healthy life up to fourteen and a half years.

Australian Champion ELLENDALE TRAVELLER (Raq)
Born 1967

Sire: Ch Greenscrees Swordsman
Dam: Ellendale Witch of Plovern
Breeder/Owner in UK: Maurice Baker
Owner in Australia: Mrs P.Y. Carpenter

A racy sable and white with a beautiful head and eye, very similar in many respects to his sire and with the same superb temperament. He took a challenge certificate at Leicester while he was still a puppy and was a most efficient stud dog from an early age. Due to business problems and a possible move, I parted with him to Pam Carpenter and he took nine challenge certificates in Australia, two in New Zealand and was also a best in show winner. Among his many winning children was the impressive Champion Anmoray Angus.

Bob Richman

Australian Champion ELLENDALE ETIENNE (Shep)
Born 1970

Sire: Ch Greenscrees Nobleman
Dam: Belle of Breconcroft
Breeder: Master A. Davis
Owner in UK: Maurice Baker
Owner in Australia: Mrs P.Y. Carpenter

A most loved dog of exactly the right size, with a great resemblance to his sire. He had a beautifully moulded head and lovely dark eye, always carried a huge coat and was a natural showman. He took a challenge certificate and reserve challenge certificate in the United Kingdom and was twice reserve best in show at Mid-Western Shetland Sheepdog Club breed open shows. I thought he should have easily gained his title here, but I lost patience and let him go to Australia – a decision I've always regretted. He became an Australian champion in four shows, won groups and best in show and was a successful sire.

Gerald Foyle

South African Champion LIRREN SHARPSHOOTER (Ross)
Born 1973

Sire: Troubleshooter of Shemaur
Dam: Lirren Black Lace
Breeder: Mrs Lin French
Owner: Mrs Avril Ventress

Ross was the first sheltie owned by Avril and was purchased as an eight week old puppy. Avril was encouraged to show him and he had some good wins in England before being taken to South Africa when his owner emigrated in 1975. He made quite an impact on his arrival and soon became the top sheltie in South Africa. He had an outstanding career both in the ring and at stud. Apart from gaining his title, he was a best in show winner and a strong contender on more than one occasion for the Dog Of The Year award.

**Australian Champion FELTHORN HARVEST MOON (Quincy)
Born 1982**

Sire: Shelbrook Moonlighting
Dam: Felthorn Marionette
Breeders: Mr and Mrs R. Thornley
Owner: Mrs Lesley Tanks

This impressive tri colour owes much of his success to the patience of his breeders. A full brother to Champion Felthorn Button Moon, Quincy was never shown as a puppy in the United Kingdom but held back to go to Australia. He fulfilled his potential down under. He was sent to Australia in 1985 at the age of two and a half and he became the quickest United Kingdom import to gain his title. On the way, he won groups and best in shows and finally proved a successful sire with champion children now beginning to emulate his success in the showring.

Michael M. Trafford

Appendices
Breed Clubs in the UK

English Shetland Sheepdog Club
Secretary: Mr R. Thornley, Pie Hatch, Brettenham Road, Buxhall, Stowmarket, Suffolk.
Telephone 04493 7729.

Mid Western Shetland Sheepdog Club
Secretary: Mrs M. Dobson, Tavistock, Clifton Village, nr Preston, Lancs PR4 0ZA.
Telephone 0772 683505.

Northern Counties Shetland Sheepdog Club
Secretary: Miss M. Gatherall, Sockburn Hall, Neasham, Darlington, Co Durham.
Telephone 060-981 293.

Yorkshire Shetland Sheepdog Club
Secretary: Mrs B. Butler, 8 Drake Close, Burncross, Sheffield S30 4TB.
Telephone 0742 462291.

Scottish Shetland Sheepdog Club
Secretary: Mrs M. Anderson, Vaila, Ayr Road, Irvine, Ayrshire.
Telephone 0294 311447.

Shetland Sheepdog Club of Wales
Secretary: Mrs V. Dyer, Hayes End, Longney, nr Gloucester GL2 6SW.
Telephone 0452 720594.

Shetland Sheepdog Club of North Wales
Secretary: Mr B. Kenny, Crisanbee, 4 Higher Road, Harmer Hill, nr Shrewsbury.
Telephone 0939 290082.

Shetland Sheepdog Club of Northern Ireland
Secretary: Mrs I. McGucken, 20 Station Road, Carnalea, Bangor, Co Down, N Ireland.
Telephone 0247 452678.

Champion Shetland Sheepdogs

Dogs which have gained their titles since 1975

Ch Balidorn White Ginger	Sable and white
Ch Beckwith Bit Of A Vagabond at Shelmyth	Tricolour
Ch Blenmerrow Brewmaster	Sable and white
Ch Blenmerrow Oak Apple	Sable and white
Ch Boomerang of Monkreddan	Sable and white
Ch Bridgedale Playboy	Sable and white
Ch Cierrhig Cragsman	Tricolour
Ch Cowellekot Crown Prince of Stormane	Sable and white
Ch Cultured at Cashella	Tricolour
Ch Drumcauchlie Bumble Boy	Tricolour
Ch Dunbeck Dancing Master	Sable and white
Ch Fairona Rockafella	Sable and white
Ch Felthorn Beachcomber	Sable and white
Ch Ferdinando of Myriehewe	Sable and white
Ch Forestland Briar	Sable and white
Ch Forestland Target	Sable and white
Ch Foxlark Fandango	Sable and white
Ch Francehill Andy Pandy	Sable and white
Ch Francehill Beach Boy	Sable and white
Ch Francehill Dollar Bid at Lochkaren	Sable and white
Ch Francehill Florentine	Sable and white
Ch Francehill Goodwill	Sable and white
Ch Francehill Persimon	Sable and white
Ch Francehill Tickled Pink	Tricolour
Ch Franwick Sun God	Sable and white
Ch Garlea Iona Lad	Sable and white
Ch Glaysdale Boy Wonder	Sable and white
Ch Glaysdale Buccaneer	Sable and white
Ch Glenamoy Silver Crusader	Blue merle
Ch Greenscrrees Rodman	Sable and white
Ch Haralice Something Swift	Sable and white
Ch Hartmere Harris Tweed	Sable and white
Ch Haytimer of Hanburyhill at Hartmere	Sable and white
Ch Herds Hurdler	Tricolour
Ch Herriot of Herds	Tricolour
Ch Imp of Lynray	Sable and white
Ch Jefsfire Jaztime	Sable and white
Ch Kamaravia Plainsman	Sable and white
Ch Leirinmore Firethorn	Sable and white
Ch Lirren Evening Shadow at Ramtin	Tricolour

Ch Longdells Petoski	Tricolour
Ch Longdells Petroceilli	Tricolour
Ch Loughrigg Kings Minstrel	Tricolour
Ch Lythwood Saga	Sable and white
Ch Lythwood Scrabble	Sable and white
Ch Lythwood Sky Master	Sable and white
Ch Lythwood Snaffels	Sable and white
Ch Lythwood Spruce	Sable and white
Ch MacIntosh of Francehill	Blue merle
Ch Marksman of Ellendale	Sable and white
Ch Marowat Master of Joywill	Sable and white
Ch Marnham The Joker	Sable and white
Ch Merry Rustler of Myriehewe	Sable and white
Ch Midnitesun Justin Time	Sable and white
Ch Mistmere Marking Time at Stornaway	Sable and white
Ch Monkredden Royal Blend	Sable and white
Ch Mountmoor Blue Boy	Blue merle
Ch Myriehewe Moonshine	Sable and white
Ch Myriehewe Spanish Galleon from Tracelyn	Sable and white
Ch Nitelife Rogue Star	Tricolour
Ch Paramali Rustler	Tricolour
Ch Penrave Private Benjamin	Tricolour
Ch Pepperhill Blue Fizz	Blue merle
Ch Pruneparks Jason Junior	Sable and white
Ch Rainelor Ranger	Sable and white
Ch Rhinog The Gay Lancer	Sable and white
Ch Rinsey Sea Marksman	Sable and white
Ch Riverhill Ricotta	Sable and white
Ch Riverhill Ring Master	Tricolour
Ch Rockaround Night Hawk	Tricolour
Ch Rosdyke Moonlight Shadow	Blue merle
Ch Ruscombe Silver Lining	Blue merle
Ch Salroyds Buzzer	Tricolour
Ch Sandpiper of Sharval	Sable and white
Ch Scarabrae Statesman	Sable and white
Ch Scylla Scottish Rifle	Sable and white
Ch Shelabane Reme Moses	Tricolour
Ch Shelderon Gay Ghillie	Sable and white
Ch Shelerts Sinbad The Sailor	Sable and white
Ch Shelerts Such A Gamble	Blue merle
Ch Shelerts Tickles My Fancy	Tricolour
Ch Shemaur Noel Edmonds	Tricolour
Ch Shetlo The Gay Piper	Sable and white
Ch Shezlyn Brown Velvet	Sable and white
Ch Snabswood Slainthe	Sable and white
Ch Stornaway Star Spangled	Blue merle
Ch Sulasgeir Talamba of Shemaur	Sable and white
Ch Tuffeigha Moonraker	Sable and white
Ch Tyeford Thoami	Sable and white
Ch Westaglow Nijinsky	Sable and white
Ch Willow Tarn Telstar	Sable and white

91 dogs — 63 sable and white, 20 tricolour, 8 blue merle.

Bitches which have gained their titles since 1975

Ch Alwillans Pink Moon	Sable and white
Ch Arcot Miss Tinna	Sable and white
Ch Banreen Na Shee	Tricolour
Ch Blue Opal of Heathlow	Blue merle
Ch Blue Spangled Ivory	Blue merle
Ch Brantcliffe Gem Of Love	Blue merle
Ch Bridgedale Bali Hi	Sable and white
Ch Bridgedale Bonny Girl	Sable and white
Ch Bridgedale Dolly Bird	Sable and white
Ch Bridgedale Lotus Blossom	Sable and white
Ch Daleoak Christmas Rose	Sable and white
Ch Dunbrae Gold 'n' Bianco	Sable and white
Ch Felthorn Button Moon	Blue merle
Ch Felthorn Lady	Blue merle
Ch Felthorn Lady Luck at Morestyle	Tricolour
Ch Forestland Tassel	Sable and white
Ch Francehill Dolly Bird	Sable and white
Ch Francehill Flora Dora	Sable and white
Ch Francehill Lotus Blossom	Sable and white
Ch Francehill Pin Up	Sable and white
Ch Franwick Sister Jane	Sable and white
Ch Glaysdale Heiress	Sable and white
Ch Glenawind Lavender Lady	Blue merle
Ch Glensanda Gems Kirsty	Tricolour
Ch Greensands Gangsters Moll of Monkswood	Tricolour
Ch Heathlake Holiday Time	Sable and white
Ch Heathlow Priscilla	Sable and white
Ch Hebson Gale Force at Hartmere	Sable and white
Ch Jasmine of Janetstown	Sable and white
Ch Jefsfire Rich Reward	Sable and white
Ch Joywill Jeaneta	Sable and white
Ch Keredian Country Gem	Sable and white
Ch Kirsty Ann of Monkreddan	Sable and white
Ch Kyleburn Athena	Tricolour
Ch Kyleburn Good Time Girl	Tricolour
Ch Kyleburn Penny Royal	Tricolour
Ch Kyleburn Razzle Dazzle	Sable and white
Ch Kyleburn Star Sound	Tricolour
Ch Kyleburn Wild Thyme	Sable and white
Ch Ladybird of Landover	Tricolour

Ch Laiderette of Kyleburn	Tricolour
Ch Larool Candyfloss of Jefsfire	Sable and white
Ch Lilt of Kyleburn	Tricolour
Ch Linvallea Ember	Sable and white
Ch Loves Folly of Diomed	Blue merle
Ch Lythwood Sandalwood	Sable and white
Ch Lythwood Sea Nymph	Sable and white
Ch Marnham Merry Maker	Sable and white
Ch Midnitesun White Heather	Sable and white
Ch Moccas Cashiered CDEX	Sable and white
Ch Mohnesee Sweet Martini	Sable and white
Ch Mohnesee Sweet Reflection	Sable and white
Ch Monkreddan Sunray	Sable and white
Ch Monkswood Girl Friday of Greensands	Sable and white
Ch Monkswood May Garland	Sable and white
Ch Monkswood Meridian	Sable and white
Ch Morlich Marie Celeste	Sable and white
Ch Mountmoor Jeanie McCall	Sable and white
Ch Myriehewe Fantasia	Sable and white
Ch Myriehewe Spanish Romance	Sable and white
Ch Myriehewe Witchcraft	Tricolour
Ch Nitelife Moonshadow	Tricolour
Ch Orean Abbalinda	Sable and white
Ch Philhope Stardust	Sable and white
Ch Rainelor Reinetta	Tricolour
Ch Rhinog How D'You Do	Sable and white
Ch Roaming of Exford	Blue merle
Ch Rockaround Crystal Charm	Blue merle
Ch Rockaround Crystal Sky	Blue merle
Ch Rodhill Clouded Dawn	Sable and white
Ch Santrev Silk Rose	Sable and white
Ch Sanvar Sunrise	Sable and white
Ch Scylla Snow Violet	Blue merle
Ch Seavall Spangle	Sable and white
Ch Sharval Merle Oberon	Blue merle
Ch Shelbrook Whispering Waves	Blue merle
Ch Shelderon Kiri	Blue merle
Ch Sheldon Valgay Vesper	Sable and white
Ch Shelert's Sands of Delight	Sable and white
Ch Shelfrect Sugar Bon Bon	Sable and white
Ch Shelmyth Sweet Expression	Sable and white
Ch Shelridge Ceilidh	Sable and white
Ch Shelverne Spun Gold	Sable and white
Ch Shetlo Sheraleigh	Sable and white
Ch Silver Lady of Stornaway	Blue merle
Ch Skerrywood Sandstorm	Sable and white
Ch Snabswood Summer Wine at Willow Tarn	Sable and white
Ch Solveig of Snabswood	Sable and white
Ch Sonymer Sheena	Sable and white
Ch Sonymer Silver Bell	Blue merle
Ch Stevlyns Carousel	Sable and white
Ch Stormane Suzette	Sable and white
Ch Stormane Shining Light	Sable and white

Ch Tarfin Cregagh Blue Melody	Blue merle
Ch True Delight at Tirrick	Sable and white
Ch Waindale Minette	Sable and white
Ch Willow Tarn Tear Maria	Sable and white
Ch Willow Tarn True Love	Sable and white

98 bitches — 67 Sable and white, 14 Tri colour, 17 Blue merle